P9-DHD-861

RE THINK
RE INVENT
RE POSITION

Medical Library
North Memorial Health Care
3300 Oakdale Avenue North
Robbinsdale, MN 55422

Medical Library
North Memorial Health Care
3300 Oakdale Avenue North
Robbinsdale, MN 55422

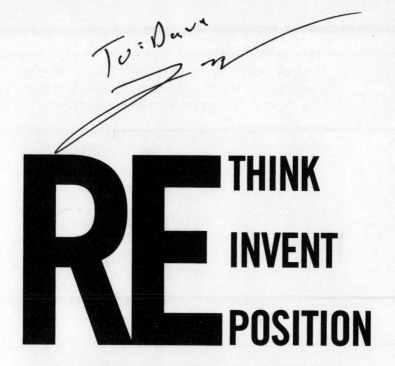

RE THINK
RE INVENT
RE POSITION

12 STRATEGIES TO RENEW YOUR BUSINESS AND BOOST YOUR BOTTOM LINE

Medical Library
North Memorial Health Care
3300 Oakdale Avenue North
Robbinsdale, MN 55422

LEO HOPF & WILLIAM WELTER

A BUSINESS

Avon, Massachusetts

Copyright © 2010 Leo Hopf and William Welter
All rights reserved.
This book, or parts thereof, may not be reproduced in any
form without permission from the publisher; exceptions are
made for brief excerpts used in published reviews.

Published by Adams Business,
an imprint of Adams Media, a division of F+W Media, Inc.
57 Littlefield Street, Avon, MA 02322. U.S.A.
www.adamsmedia.com

ISBN 10: 1-60550-024-0
ISBN 13: 978-1-60550-024-9
eISBN 10: 1-4405-0716-3
eISBN 13: 978-1-4405-0716-8

Printed in the United States of America.

10 9 8 7 6 5 4 3 2 1

Library of Congress Cataloging-in-Publication Data
is available from the publisher.

This publication is designed to provide accurate and authoritative information with regard to the subject matter covered. It is sold with the understanding that the publisher is not engaged in rendering legal, accounting, or other professional advice. If legal advice or other expert assistance is required, the services of a competent professional person should be sought.
—From a *Declaration of Principles* jointly adopted by a
Committee of the American Bar Association and
a Committee of Publishers and Associations

Many of the designations used by manufacturers and sellers to distinguish their product are claimed as trademarks. Where those designations appear in this book and Adams Media was aware of a trademark claim, the designations have been printed with initial capital letters.

This book is available at quantity discounts for bulk purchases.
For information, please call 1-800-289-0963.

DEDICATION

Leo dedicates this book to Harriet and Eileen—you are the reason I get on the plane and why I'm delighted to come home again.

Bill dedicates this book to the men and women of the United States Marine Corps—always adapting—always renewing—always faithful. *Semper Fi!*

ACKNOWLEDGMENTS

We would like to acknowledge the following "thought partners" who helped us form the ideas embedded in this book: Jon Atchue; Kevin Baartman; John Bakke; Mary Bober; Deanna Brady; Mary Carter; Walt Catlow; Ben Chortkoff; Susan Chortkoff; Bob Clarke; Nora Collins; Phil Donaldson; Amy Frasier; Dennis Goettsch; Harriet Hopf, MD; Peter Hsia; Scott Jacobson; Jessica Lamker; Tres Lund; Darcy Stivland; Steve MacGill; Ed Mason; Jean Delaney Nelson; David Miller; Scott Peterson; Mary Kay Plantes; Burke Robinson; Kavah Safavi, MD, JD; Brad Shorr; Ginny Steele; Bill Talbot; Larry Voeller; and Warren Zaccaro.

We would also like to thank Milt and Edie Chortkoff, George Harad, Kim Wirthlin, and Michael Shader for their help in developing case studies.

Finally, we would like to gratefully acknowledge the help of our agent, Lisa Adams, and our editor, Peter Archer, in bringing this book from concept to reality.

Contents

INTRODUCTION

This is a book about the reality of business lifecycles and focuses on one of the hardest decisions a business leader has to make. Like it or not, every product, every service, every business, every company will eventually mature and go into decline. It may not be happening to you now and may not happen soon—but it will happen unless you decide to proactively renew your business. This maturity or decline will bring you to a decision that many leaders hope to avoid—what to do with a business that is no longer as relevant and vital as it once was.

All products, services, and lines of business have a lifecycle. Businesses are launched, some survive, and some die quickly. Those that survive grow modestly or spectacularly and then inevitably mature. Some remain mature for a long time while others pass into decline more quickly. Managers tend to think of the business lifecycle as a fixed path that can be stretched, but not fundamentally altered. They think that once a business starts its decline, the good times have come to an end.

But what if you looked on the mature phase of the lifecycle as an opportunity? What if you could see this as a point of significant renewal and the creation of a successful new future?

A Business Reality: Lifecycles Are Destiny

The lifecycle curve with its stages of innovation, growth, maturity, and decline is familiar to most businesspeople.

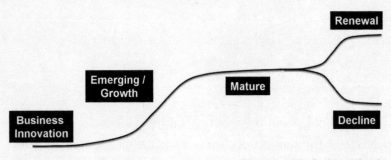

Renewal and the Business Lifecycle

Over the past ten years there has been no hotter topic than business innovation. In the late 1990s executives and business writers were sure the Internet would change everything and billions of dollars of equity were poured into ideas for "new economy" businesses. Companies in all industries invested additional billions of dollars in corporate venturing. And lately, we have been chasing the Holy Grail of "disruptive innovation," improvements that are simpler or cheaper than current offerings and that upset the status quo of a marketplace or industry. Volumes have been written on how to transform an idea for a new product, service, or business model into a viable and ongoing business.

The emerging growth stage has also been well covered by the business press. Geoffrey Moore's Chasm Group, for example, has written multiple books on the finding and winning of the "headpin" customer, the key to success for a business entering this fast-growth stage. Once the headpin has been won, Moore lays out the path for leveraging this relationship to make additional sales and accelerate growth.

As well, there are endless streams of ideas about how to run mature product lines, businesses, and companies. From line extensions to geographic expansion to Continuous Improvement to Six Sigma to Lean, there is no shortage of suggestions about how to make these businesses more efficient and effective in order to extend their useful life.

Surprisingly, however, there is comparatively little guidance as to how to rethink, reinvent, and reposition an ongoing business. That underserved topic is the focus of this book.

This is a book for the leaders who will be driving renewal efforts. You might be a CEO or a director renewing a company; a senior vice president renewing a division; a vice president renewing a business unit; or a director renewing a product line. Or you might be a small- or medium-sized business owner who has to do the heavy lifting by yourself. Whatever the case, the responsibility for renewal rests with you and your team.

Managers and leaders of organizations understand how to deal with the risks in running their business, but renewal is very different. Consider a basic definition of risk: the probability that exposure to a hazard will lead to a negative consequence. Risk is inherent in renewal. If renewal is to take place, the leader of the organization must willingly expose him or herself to some possibility of absolute failure. Renewal is not for the faint-hearted. Many executives are willing to risk their company's money; fewer are willing to risk their own reputation.

Renewal can't be done on the side or part-time. It cannot be handed to a team of lower-level managers. Either you are going to lead the effort or it's not going to get done. In this book we will arm you with the tools, processes, and examples you require for successful renewal. You already know how to run your business. We will provide what you need to renew it.

Renewing a Business Is Not the Same as Running It

All your past experience and instincts about how to run a business will almost assuredly be *wrong* when it comes to renewal. Renewing a business is not even close to business as usual. Consider the following regarding the three main stages of business growth and maturity:

- During the **Business Innovation** phase you are typically taking relatively small risks that involve only a tiny part of the larger organization. The scale is small, and failure, though regrettable, is not significantly damaging. You will see tremendous upside for any of the risks that pay off, and relatively small downside for those that do not. But when you renew a business, you are making substantial changes to the engines that deliver a large part of your revenues and net income, that define your brand and market positioning, and that employ the vast majority of your assets and workforce.
- During the **Emerging Growth** phase you have an idea that has been proven in one market and you are now expanding it to new customers, industries, and geographies. But during renewal you will have already accessed the markets within your grasp. Now, as your opportunities begin to shrink, you must think of how to revitalize your offerings to make them more attractive to customers.
- During the **Mature** phase you focus on efficiency and delivering what was promised. Predictability and continuous

improvement are the keys to success. But to renew a business you must by necessity take risks that are much larger than those taken day-to-day. Not all of these risks will succeed.

No Business Grows Forever, but There Are Always Growth Businesses

Leaders know when their businesses are not performing at the level required. They feel something should be done, but few have the will, the clarity, and the alignment to truly renew their company, division, business unit, or product line. So while some leaders successfully renew their business, and others try and fail, most never even make the attempt. They keep operating their businesses as they have always done and sentence them to inevitable decline.

Sometimes the decline is slow; sometimes, as during a shift in basic technology, the decline is swift. This is hardly new. Shifts in basic technology were considered by the economist Joseph Schumpeter when he wrote about "the winds of creative destruction" in the 1940s. Markets don't wait for industry leaders to give them approval to change. They change at the rate of consumer acceptance—which is often much faster than the reaction time of the industry's competitors.

Consider Polaroid. They were the technology leader for decades and had a strong-selling digital camera for the 1999 Christmas season—but they pulled it from the market because it interfered with what they saw as their primary business—the sale of film. Film was where they made their "real money." They may have worried about their decline, but they took no real action to renew their business. They were so focused on their film sales that they could not make the switch to filmless digital cameras in time to be a player in the new industry.

Some companies recognize the necessity of renewal but wait too long and then find themselves whipsawed by market forces. Had they acted sooner they might have been able to renew their business and position themselves for success—but they missed their chance and let other companies take the initiative.

Look at Yahoo! They made numerous acquisitions unrelated to their basic search engine product. Meanwhile Google rolled out new products and continued to refine its link-based search engine. Once the market leader in search engine technology, Yahoo! searches have plummeted to less than 25 percent of Google's. After turning down an acquisition offer of $33 per share by Microsoft in May 2008 (Yahoo! was holding out for $37 per share), Yahoo!'s stock price dropped below $10 per share within the year.

And to add insult to injury, Microsoft introduced its own search competitor (Bing), which promptly ate into Yahoo!'s remaining searches. Less than three months after Bing was launched Microsoft and Yahoo! agreed on a ten-year joint search agreement that replaces Yahoo!'s search engine with Bing. This deal effectively removes Yahoo! from the search game and has them selling advertising instead.

Renewal is seldom easy and carries more risk of outright failure in the near-term than riding the business through maturity and into decline. But it also offers the possibility of meaningful reward. Businesses that successfully renew enjoy the levels of growth and margins that restore them to a valued position in a company's overall portfolio.

How Do You Know When It Is Time to Renew a Business?

Virtually all organizations have metrics for determining the health of their day-to-day business. But how do you determine if it is time to renew the business? With our framework and your judgment you will be able to choose which businesses should be renewed and which should continue under their current direction.

We have developed a list of leading indicators to help you tell when you are nearing the time to renew your business. We've grouped these indicators into seven categories. They are:

1. Senior leadership
2. Business metrics
3. Customer base
4. Industry and competition
5. Workforce
6. Leadership
7. Gut feel

First and most importantly, is **senior leadership** dissatisfied with the status quo and are they ready for something else? If senior leadership is unwilling to consider significant changes to the business model, any renewal effort will be doomed to failure before it has even begun.

Second, look at important **business metrics**. Examine your business objectively. Is revenue growth slowing, and are you under margin pressure? These are signs a business is losing its way in the marketplace. If you are a retailer or restaurant business with multiple stores, are you seeing a steady decline in same-store sales? This could be a sign of growing stale, or more importantly, a sign that your business is becoming irrelevant.

Do you see the beginnings of consolidation in your industry? Have there been any recent "breakthrough" products or services? Are you picking up ground on the competition, staying even, or losing out?

Third, consider your **customer base**. Do you see interest drifting away from your offerings? Are your best customers going elsewhere, and do you find it harder to acquire new customers?

Your customers' demands are not static but change over time. Are they transforming faster than you are able to adapt? During a conversation, a store manager of a major "old line" retailer in Florida told us that "our best customers are dying faster than we are attracting new customers." Now this is an unambiguous call for renewal!

Prior to the 2009 recession, many organizations assumed the Boomer generation would spend every dime they made (and then some). However, during the recession the Boomers suddenly took their savings from less than 1 percent of income to 5 percent of income—pulling billions of dollars from consumption. Businesses have been scrambling to cope with this new pattern of customer spending. This is the sort of unpredicted shift in consumer behavior that should cause businesses to examine the case for renewal.

Next, take a broader look at your **industry and competition**. Most organizations have a pretty good feel for their traditional competitors. But what about new companies that don't look like you and that compete very differently? Starbucks didn't look like Folgers, so for a long time Folgers didn't accept them as a serious competitor. Until it was too late, of course. Folgers assumed that their main competitors were the companies that sold coffee through grocery stores. They missed a fundamental shift in consumer behavior, as more and more people began drinking their coffee on the run, stopping by Starbucks to grab a latte.

Is your entire industry reeling under the impact of shocks that are invalidating traditional assumptions? Blockbuster knew people would drive to pick up their movies to watch at home. That was fine until Netflix and video-on-demand eliminated the need to ever leave the house.

Now look closer to home and consider your **workforce**. Are the number and quality of ideas coming from your employees slowing down? Has the level of enthusiasm of your best performers changed? Are your best people leaving in search of better opportunities elsewhere?

The sixth category is **leadership**, and we suggest that you start with the relationship between the leaders and the workforce in your company. Do the employees have confidence in the ability of the leaders to turn things around? And over time is their confidence growing or waning?

Another leadership issue you must evaluate is your attitude toward risk. For a variety of reasons, leaders often have difficulty in taking the risks necessary to renew their businesses. This is especially true when previous attempts at renewal have failed.

In many businesses we see smart decisions blocked by the weight of history. A product line may be held beyond its useful life so as not to offend its creator. Or a business location may have an emotional significance even though the demographics of the neighborhood have changed.

And often leaders regard short-term results as more important than long-term business health.

For each of these problems, you must examine your ability to meet the challenge and overcome it. And that means being completely honest with yourself and your leadership team.

The seventh category to consider is the most personal of all—your **gut feel** about the business and renewal.

Sometimes we find that owners and leaders begin to find their pasts more attractive than their futures. Instead of looking forward to the excitement of tomorrow's challenges, they drain their energy by simply running their businesses.

Their guts are telling them something that their heads refuse to believe. They commiserate with friends over the dreadful state of the industry but deny the need to renew *their* businesses. They substitute cheerleading for the hard questioning and planning that will lead to an attractive future.

Renewal Checklist

To determine whether or not your business is in need of renewal we have created a renewal checklist. You can apply it to your company, division, business unit, or product line. Better yet, have your entire leadership team take the assessment independently and compare scores and observations. We have done this many times and find it triggers conversations that will help in your renewal efforts.

Consider the following list and rate your business on each of the items. We consider the first item a bellwether item, and therefore weight it more heavily than the rest. Score it zero points for "not like us," five points for "kind of like us," and ten points if "just like us." The rest of the items should be scored as follows: one point for "not like us," two points for "kind of like us," and three points for "just like us."

ORGANIZATIONAL READINESS
1. Senior leadership is dissatisfied with the status quo and is ready to try something else.

BUSINESS METRICS
1. Revenue growth is slowing.
2. Margin pressure is unrelenting.
3. Same store sales are declining.
4. We've had few breakthrough offerings recently.
5. Our industry is consolidating.

CUSTOMERS
1. Customer interest is drifting away from our offerings.
2. Our biggest/best customers are shopping around.
3. We are winning new customers more slowly.
4. Customer demographics are changing faster than we are.
5. Our customers are facing structural changes and pressures.

INDUSTRY AND COMPETITION
1. Our industry is shrinking.
2. Our industry is described in the media as old, tired, or slow.
3. Organizations that compete differently are winning business from us.

4. Shocks to our industry are invalidating traditional assumptions.
5. We are lagging the trends in our industry.

WORKFORCE
1. We are getting fewer and fewer ideas from our employees.
2. We are losing the enthusiasm of our best performers.
3. We have slowed hiring, and our workforce is aging.
4. We find it harder to recruit top talent.
5. Our people are leaving in search of better opportunities elsewhere.

LEADERSHIP
1. People are losing confidence that our leaders can turn things around.
2. Smart decisions are routinely blocked by the weight of history.
3. Existing leaders won't take the necessary risks to renew the business.
4. Previous attempts at fixing the business have failed.
5. Delivering short-term results overrides creating long-term business health.

GUT FEEL
1. Our past feels more attractive than our future.
2. The business drains our energy rather than energizes us.
3. We commiserate with others about our business rather than brag about it.

4. It takes regular cheerleading to keep people excited about the business.
5. We have lost interest in running the business.

Add up your points, remembering that item 1 is weighted heavier than the others.

- *Less than fifty points:* Your business should focus on continuous improvement along your current path.
- *Fifty to seventy-five points:* You should consider your business for the renewal watch list.
- *Seventy-five or more points:* Your business urgently needs renewal, and needs it now.

Structure of the Book

We have identified twelve distinctive strategies for proactive business renewal. Each strategy corresponds to a different combination of customers and assets. The twelve strategies have different risk and reward characteristics, and each has its own requirements for success. We will discuss each of the twelve and their implications and will help you determine which one best matches your needs.

In addition, we will describe the levers you can use to adjust your business model and how you can use them to shift from your current strategy to the renewal strategy you select. We will also describe an effective and efficient process for driving renewal within your organization.

There are three phases in the renewal process: Rethink, Reinvent, and Reposition. **Rethinking** answers the question as to whether the business needs renewal or whether it should continue operating under the current model. **Reinventing** is the creation of the new business model that will provide an attractive future for the business. And **Repositioning** is the action of transitioning from the old business model to the new one.

Chapter 1 provides an overview of the twelve strategies for business renewal, which are the core of this book. Chapter 2 outlines the Rethink, Reinvent, and Reposition process for renewing your business. Reading these chapters will give you the big picture of business renewal.

Chapters 3 through 8 provide the tools and frameworks for doing the work of business renewal. Each of these chapters expands on one part of the renewal process. Chapter 3 focuses on Rethinking your portfolio to identify possible renewal candidates. Chapter 4 focuses on what it takes to obtain organizational commitment to a renewal effort. Chapter 5 covers Reinvention and describes how to build a powerful set of alternatives for your business. Chapter 6 is a deep dive into the twelve strategies, describing how they are different, how they can be applied, and offering examples of companies that have used each of the twelve. Chapter 7 covers what must be done to achieve agreement within the organization on the selected strategy. And Chapter 8 describes what it takes to Reposition a business to make the transition from the current model to the new model.

Chapter 9 presents common traps found during renewal efforts and how to avoid them. Finally, Chapter 10 considers the reality of having to prepare the organization, especially the young leaders, to meet future renewal challenges.

And if you are interested in continuing the conversation after reading the book, go to our blog at *www.rethinkreinvent reposition.com* where you can submit questions to us directly and learn from the experiences of other readers.

Now, let's move on to an overview of the twelve strategies.

CHAPTER ONE

Twelve Strategies for Organizational Renewal

Before beginning our journey, we have to know the destination. Our objective is for you to successfully execute a renewal strategy that creates a growing and profitable future for your organization.

The way to reach this goal is by applying one of twelve renewal strategies to your business. These are not one-size-fits-all strategies. Each must be tailored to fit the needs at hand. Exclude those that are obviously inappropriate to your situation and choose from the remaining ones that seem closest to your needs. Then tailor your chosen strategy to meet your specific requirements. In this way, you will be able to efficiently and effectively create a strategy that is right for you.

This chapter provides an overview of the twelve basic strategies, along with a handful of examples to show how they've worked in practice. We'll undertake a deeper explanation of each strategy in Chapter 6.

What Drives the Twelve Strategies?

All businesses, large or small, public or private, selling products or services, face the reality of lifecycle maturity and decline. In preparing this book, we wanted to make its lessons apply as broadly as possible. We finally boiled it down to the root question: *"What do all businesses have in common?"*

The answers are straightforward:

1. All companies have customers who purchase their goods and services to satisfy their needs.
2. All companies have assets (both hard and soft) they use to create these offerings.

Customer relationships and assets take time to build and require focus and investment to maintain. By examining different combinations of customer needs and company assets we developed the twelve strategies.

Sometimes customer needs are long-lived. Cooks have needed salt for all of recorded history, and in the industrialized world oil has been a mainstay of commerce for over 100 years. But more often (and increasingly so), the time from the introduction of an offering to the end of its profitable life is getting shorter. For example, companies needed "Y2K" expertise for 1999 and not much beyond that. Only a decade ago, people could make a decent living manufacturing and repairing video cassette recorders. Today, VCRs have been supplanted by digital recording devices. Customers' needs evolve, and if you don't match them, your formerly attractive offerings become obsolete.

Assets, too, may have a long or short life. Andersen Corporation opened its Menomonie, Wisconsin, manufacturing facility in 1904, and it is still producing top-quality windows there today. On the other hand, Intel's semiconductor chip fabrication plants cost more than $1 billion to build and will be obsolete within a decade.

A firm's hard assets are easy to see. But its soft assets are much more difficult to visualize. A company's soft assets are found in the interaction among the design engineers, the manufacturing personnel, the equipment, the suppliers, and so on. The soft assets reside in the skills, knowledge, attitude, and culture of the people in the organization.

The Twelve Strategies

The twelve strategies are driven by different combinations of customers and assets, as shown in the chart below.

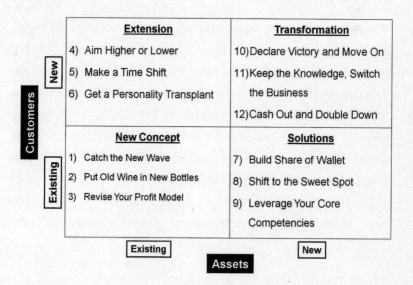

		Extension	Transformation
Customers	**New**	4) Aim Higher or Lower 5) Make a Time Shift 6) Get a Personality Transplant	10) Declare Victory and Move On 11) Keep the Knowledge, Switch the Business 12) Cash Out and Double Down
	Existing	**New Concept** 1) Catch the New Wave 2) Put Old Wine in New Bottles 3) Revise Your Profit Model	**Solutions** 7) Build Share of Wallet 8) Shift to the Sweet Spot 9) Leverage Your Core Competencies
		Existing	**New**
		Assets	

For clarity's sake, we've divided the twelve strategies into four groups of three strategies each. The four groups are:

1. **New Concept** (Catch the New Wave; Put Old Wine in New Bottles; Revise Your Profit Model).
2. **Extension** (Aim Higher or Lower; Make a Time Shift; Get a Personality Transplant).
3. **Solutions** (Build Share of Wallet; Shift to the Sweet Spot; Leverage Your Core Competencies).
4. **Transformation** (Declare Victory and Move On; Keep the Knowledge, Switch the Business; Cash Out and Double Down).

Let's examine each group in detail.

New Concept Group
(Existing Customers / Existing Assets)

If you can repurpose your existing assets to address different needs within your current customer base, you may be able to create a new concept at relatively low risk. The challenge of New Concept strategies is to make sure the change is significant enough that customers recognize what you are doing and react to it. Too often people try one of the three New Concept strategies and end up modestly changing their business model in a way that is insufficient to truly renew the business.

How Can We Renew Our Business?	Description	Topics to Consider
Catch the New Wave	Shift your current business to the next hot thing.	You look at your market and see both emergence and obsolescence. New customer wants and needs are replacing those you have satisfied in the past. How can you identify and jump to the next new thing?
Put Old Wine in New Bottles	Repackage/rebrand your offerings to make them seem fresh and original.	Your underlying offerings still provide value to customers. How can you make offerings that have been around for a long time seem fresh and new?
Revise Your Profit Model	If the way you are charging for your products and services is no longer effective, find other ways to generate revenue and profits.	You look at the marketplace and see value migrating away from your current profit model. How can you structure your model differently to accelerate growth and increase profitability?

STRATEGY 1: CATCH THE NEW WAVE

CASE STUDY For most of us, getting our clothes dry cleaned is as exciting and rewarding as taking out the trash. Dry cleaning is just something that has to be done every week or two; at best, you will get your clothes back as they were so you can start the cycle again. Most people look at dropping off dry cleaning as a necessary evil to be done with the least hassle and annoyance possible.

Hassle and annoyance are what we associate with dry cleaning if we think about it at all. "Honey, did you remember to pick up the dry cleaning?" "What do you mean it is not ready?" "The button was on the shirt when I dropped it off!" "I'm sorry, dear. I know your flight is Monday morning, but it is Sunday and the dry cleaner isn't open."

Unless, that is, they live in Burbank, California, where Milt & Edie's Dry Cleaners is located. Milt & Edie's has defined the new wave in dry cleaning and in so doing turned it from an annoyance into a pleasure. Most dry cleaners think of their industry in terms of plant throughput; Milt & Edie's think in terms of service.

Here is what happens at Milt & Edie's. You arrive in the spacious parking lot at any time. They are open twenty-four hours a day, seven days a week. Music is playing, and you pass a koi pond on the way in. You smell the complimentary popcorn and cookies as you enter. You are greeted at the door (usually by name) and directed to one of the nine fully staffed counters.

Every single item of your clothing is inspected as it is cleaned. If you have a loose button or torn pocket, one of their seven tailors will fix it free of charge. The tailors will also make more significant repairs such as mending a ripped sleeve. When you pick your clothes up you will be told of the repair and asked if you choose to pay for it. Virtually everyone gladly pays for the repairs, but you have the right to say no since you did not ask them to do the work; they just did it for you.

Your clothes come back in better shape than you left them. You receive friendly, personalized service. You are treated as a valued customer and hailed by name. If Milt & Edie's was in your neighborhood, what reason would you have for not giving them your business?

Milt & Edie's serves the same customers from the same location with the same building and other major assets as they always have. But by pushing the service envelope the company has created a new wave. They put the "Wow" in dry cleaning.

Successful businesses don't just stand still; they follow customer tastes. Today a restaurateur may be opening an Italian pasta bar, while tomorrow it will change to a Mexican taco stand. The building and equipment for a restaurant are pretty much the same, no matter while kind of cuisine it serves.

The difference between success and failure as you switch from one kind of restaurant to another may not be in the physical assets as much as in your brand, your knowledge assets, and your reputation. Does your chef know Mexican food as well as she knows Italian food? Will customers flock to the trendy new Mexican spot if it's still called Luigi's?

Lettuce Entertain You in Chicago has been on the leading edge of food trends and they have a loyal following. Their organization makes tough decisions regularly, and mature restaurant concepts are killed off to make room for fresh new ones. Their continuous search for new ideas has brought over thirty different restaurant concepts to the market. Among these are Big Bowl (Chinese/Thai), Nacional 27 (Central and South American), and Tru (French.)

STRATEGY 2: PUT OLD WINE IN NEW BOTTLES

CASE STUDY The University of Utah is held in high esteem by Utahns. But over time the university's health care brand had fractured into many pieces as individual services went their own way. These services had developed their own, sometimes conflicting, brand images.

The result was more than sixty different logos and inconsistent use of names within the university health care system. Because the institution didn't present a unified face to the market, people didn't know which health care services were university affiliated and which were not. The absence of a unified brand made it impossible for people to say what was distinctive about the university health care system, and what set it apart from other health care providers.

The challenge, therefore, was to get the physicians who were running the different groups to agree on a single brand and logo. Most of them agreed in the abstract but resisted changing to any logo but their own. Others were not convinced that a university-wide health care would be any more effective than any of the individual service brands.

Anyone who has dealt with physicians knows that they like to tell other people what to do. They're less keen on being told that they themselves must change. How do you build a commitment to standardized branding among people who resist authority?

The university formed a team and began doing research within and outside of the university community. They conducted phone surveys and focus groups with patients, but they also interviewed the governor of Utah, a high official in the Mormon church, and health care and insurance CEOs and presidents. They also carried out a statewide survey of users.

At the start of the survey, interviewees were asked where they would like to receive their health care. They were then informed of the different pieces that made up the university system. Many were surprised at the extent and reach of the system. At the end of the interview the participants asked again, "Where would you like to receive your health care?" Once people understood the system as a whole there was a 15 percent increase in the number who said they would prefer to use the university's health care system.

The university researchers also put all of the different logos on a computer screen together with logos from different industries. Survey participants were then asked to pick out which of the logos were health care related and, of those, which service each logo represented.

Eighty-five percent correctly recognized the red "U" and caduceus (the staff with two intertwined serpents) logo that was being used by a few services. Almost no one recognized individual logos for the different services. Participants identified only two as health care related, and of those the recognition rate was comparatively low.

In the end, confronted with the results of this systematic research, the physicians came to an agreement. The Red U and caduceus became the centerpiece of the unified University of Utah Health Services brand identity and logo.

By putting Old Wine in New Bottles the University of Utah was able to bring all of its branding and logos under a single format, which is now recognized and respected by the marketplace. Their product had always been fine. The challenge was to make it seem fresh and compelling to patients and the surrounding community.

The key to this strategy is to recognize that while your products and services may still be delivering value, you need to find a new way to present them to your customers. By finding a new, innovative way to brand and represent their offerings, many organizations have been able to find new life and energy.

All across the country, symphony orchestras have been struggling to fill their seats and connect with new audiences. Those who love classical music continue to attend and support their local symphonies, but even these people are not always interested in an evening of classical music. Sometimes they prefer lighter, more popular fare.

To address this, many orchestras, most notably Boston's Symphony Orchestra, have created a Pops series. These use the talent of the orchestras' musicians to serve many of the same customers but do so in a way that makes the performances more accessible for the casual concert attendee.

In the world of professional sports, many teams are upgrading their stadiums. This improves the fan experience and sells high-priced luxury boxes at the same time. The same fans watch the same teams play the same sport, but they're doing it in a new environment. Examples include the San Francisco Giants baseball team, which moved from cold and windy Candlestick Park to the beautiful waterfront AT&T (formerly PacBell) Park. The Dallas Cowboys football franchise recently completed the construction of a new 80,000-seat stadium at the cost of more than $1 billion.

STRATEGY 3: REVISE YOUR PROFIT MODEL

CASE STUDY Seldom would anyone look to the United States Postal Service (USPS) for thought leadership. Over 750,000 people work for the post office, and it is renowned for its bureaucracy and reviled for its customer service.

Nimble competitors such as Federal Express (FedEx) and United Parcel Service (UPS) have profitably siphoned off huge parts of the postal business. Federal Express's motto is: "When it absolutely, positively has to get there overnight." While, in contrast, USPS says Priority Mail will be delivered in "one to three days."

Besides competition from FedEx and UPS, in recent years USPS has faced an increasing challenge from the Internet. People are doing more by e-mail and sending fewer letters via "snail mail." First Class mailing volume has been on the decline since 2002 and is unlikely to come back. Given this dire competitive and market outlook, the post office needed to change something.

In the past when a consumer wanted to ship a box via USPS he sealed it, using the proper tape, measuring each dimension, and checked it against arcane tables to find size surcharges. Finally, he weighed it to calculate postage, added stamps, waited in line at the post office, and handed over the package to be mailed.

But in 2009 USPS introduced small, medium, and large flat-rate boxes. No measuring of dimensions. No weighing. As long as you can close the box you can squeeze as much into it as you want. You can use these boxes for domestic or international mailing (though the cost is more for international mail and includes some weight limits).

Conveniently, boxes can be ordered online and delivered to your door. After you pack them, USPS will schedule a free pickup at your location.

By revising their profit model and going from price by weight to a fixed rate regardless of weight USPS has made itself more convenient and cost effective than UPS or FedEx for many types of mailing. Their service didn't speed up. Other than adding the pickup option it really hasn't changed at all. But by revising their profit model to make it more convenient for customers, USPS has made a surprisingly good attempt at renewal at a hard time in a difficult industry.

The Revise Your Profit Model strategy allows your company to retain its products and services and its customer base. What changes is not so much what you make money on, but how you generate that profit.

For example, the newspaper industry is not a happy place to be these days. Many papers have gone bankrupt (*Rocky Mountain News* in Denver), gone Internet only (*Seattle Post-Intelligencer*), or cut back on days of operation (*Detroit News*). From major cities having multiple competing papers just a few years ago, we've arrived at a point at which many in the industry expect even major cities to be without a single local paper within the coming months and years.

To address the precipitous drop-off in readership of paper editions (and the associated decline in advertising revenue) newspapers have gone to online editions in an attempt to derive revenue in a different way for the work they do. The challenge, of course, is getting people to pay for this online access.

The *New York Times* had an online subscription fee, dropped it, and is now bringing it back. Their new membership plans (Gold and Silver) will include material not available on the free site, such as behind the scenes tours and exclusive videos. On the other hand, papers with less clout will need to rely more on online advertising rather than fees for their additional revenue. It will be interesting to watch newspapers in the coming years as they attempt to fix a profit model that has been broken by technology.

Amazon offers another example of changing your profit model. The company has generated excitement with the introduction of its Kindle reader and electronic books. The Kindle's profit model is different from the one Amazon uses to sell printed books. Instead of charging $25 for a physical book, Amazon charges $250 for a Kindle 2 and $10 for each downloaded book. This revised profit model takes advantage of new technology and the increasing emphasis on "sustainability." It also does away with shipping costs and promises the customer instant gratification, since it takes far less time to download a book to the Kindle than to receive one through the mail.

Extension Group (New Customers / Existing Assets)

Extension strategies use existing assets to serve new customers by employing those assets differently. Extension is not just about reusing existing capabilities but is also about defining new processes, delivery mechanisms, and standards.

The following table summarizes the three Extension strategies.

How Can We Renew Our Business?	Description	Topics to Consider
Aim Higher or Lower	Move significantly up-market or down-market to serve customers you previously did not reach.	You may find that your existing niche is too confining or too expensive at the very time your customers are becoming thrifty. What opportunities are there for moving above or below your current positioning?
Make a Time Shift	Do business during a new or different part of the day to reach different customers.	The world really does run 24/7, so why not take advantage of it? Leverage your investments in hard and soft assets when they normally would be at rest and useless.
Get a Personality Transplant	Focus on new and emerging end-user needs.	What are the existing needs of our end users? How are their needs changing? How quickly are they changing? How can you change to be aligned with the evolving needs of your customers?

STRATEGY 4: AIM HIGHER OR LOWER

CASE STUDY Toyota came on the American scene in 1958, although it had competed in Japan from the mid-1930s. Like nearly all Japanese manufacturers, the company overcame an early reputation for poor quality, and by the mid-1980s it was producing very high-quality, middle-of-the-road automobiles—that is, solid cars for middle-class America. It quickly took market share from GM, Ford, and Chrysler then shifted its thinking to the higher-margin, upscale market players such as Mercedes.

Toyota had two "luxury" brands, the Cressida and Crown, but sales were weak at best. People thought of Toyota as solely a solid, middle-class car. In 1985, the company began market research for a new brand, the upscale Lexus, with an eye toward combining Mercedes-like luxury and Toyota reliability. Lexus was successfully launched in 1989 with the LS400 and has become a well-respected premium brand that has effectively challenged Mercedes in the United States.

Physically, a top-end Toyota is almost indistinguishable from a low-end Lexus. But the customer experience is entirely different. Lexus customers receive a substantially higher level of service than do Toyota customers. In creating the Lexus brand, Toyota could not just shift over their existing workforce to create and service their new products. They needed to raise the bar on their service level; to that end, they required new systems, training, and cost/benefit trade-offs.

In the early 2000s Toyota aimed lower and rolled out the Scion brand, targeting the youth of America. Its sales to this market were disappointing, but the cars turned out to appeal to older drivers who wanted to appear more "youthful." Toyota will continue to build its brand among young people, who will be in the market for a very long time. Meanwhile they will happily sell to customers who want to recapture their youth.

Toyota determined there was a segment of the higher-end market it could capture through careful research and brand development. There are numerous examples of companies producing an up-market product or service as a means to expand their customer base.

Going downscale also can work. BMW Group is seeing the target market for its flagship brand shrink, but the target market for its Mini is growing substantially. Mini buyers are typically younger and less affluent then BMW buyers, but they may become tomorrow's BMW customers. In the same manner, Swiss watchmakers rejuvenated their entire industry with the introduction of the low-end Swatch.

STRATEGY 5: MAKE A TIME SHIFT

CASE STUDY For much of its fifty-plus-year history, McDonald's restaurants were a lunch destination. Hamburger, fries, and a Coke; thank you very much! It wasn't until 1962 that the company introduced indoor seating, and throughout the 1960s most McDonald's restaurants didn't even open until 11:00 A.M.

In 1970 one of the company's franchisees experimented with a breakfast item: a sandwich with an egg on it. He wanted to see if he could attract customers to his restaurant during the morning hours. Ray Kroc, the founder of McDonald's, liked the sandwich, and the idea for the Egg McMuffin was born. The company expanded its menu board, and by 1976 McDonald's offered a full breakfast menu across all of its restaurants, giving it a nearly ten-year headstart on its competition as a breakfast destination.

People get hungry at all times of the day; McDonald's was smart enough to see this as an opportunity to make money. Moreover, it was able to make this change with minimal retraining of its staff and retooling of its existing physical assets.

People are hungry at lunch—give them lunch food. People are hungry in the morning—give them breakfast food. What if people get hungry between lunch and dinner? McDonalds rolled out "Snack Wraps" in 2006 to tide its customers over. What if people want a treat around mid-morning? In 2009, McDonalds provided McCafe premium coffee as the answer.

When would your customers use your products or services if you made them available? Are you there when they need you? The Make a Time Shift strategy offers you a way to expand your base without changing your location, product or service, or brand identity. Instead, you have to anticipate what your customers want, and when they want it.

Consider television schedules. It seems hard to believe now, but at one time if you wanted to watch a program on TV you would have to adjust *your* schedule to watch it when it was being broadcast. If you weren't there at the appointed hour, you missed it.

With digital video recorders (DVRs) and video-on-demand services, programming now adapts to *your* schedule. This has been great for consumers and businesses such as TiVo, which has created an entire industry based on the idea of time shifting. Cable companies such as Comcast have come out with their own DVR boxes to compete in this new time-shift industry. The traditional television networks have struggled to meet the needs of viewers who want to watch their shows when they want to watch them, not when the programs happen to be broadcast.

The movie industry has made a similar time shift. Summer blockbusters used to open on Fridays. So if you wanted to be among the first to see a film you would have to duck out of work to catch an 11:15 A.M. matinee.

Now big-budget movies open on Wednesday or Thursday at one minute after midnight. This creates an event—lines, noise, and an enthusiastic crowd experience that can be shared with friends and then bragged about through bleary eyes the next day. This time shift has meant that avid fans no longer have to sneak out for a guilty pleasure, but can instead enjoy a memorable outing with their friends. The change has also created more revenue for Regal and the other theater chains who have followed Make a Time Shift.

STRATEGY 6: GET A PERSONALITY TRANSPLANT

CASE STUDY General Motors certainly has received its share of disrespect over the past ten years or so. However, one GM brand has done a stellar job of getting a personality transplant.

Picture the typical driver of Coupe de Ville, Eldorado, Fleetwood, or Seville. You probably imagine an older, slower Cadillac driver. Now conjure up a picture of the driver of an Allanté, and you see an aggressive, hit-the-road-running driver.

Finally, picture the driver of a CTS or an Escalade. She or he is younger and every bit as hip as a "foreign" luxury-car driver. What happened? How did Cadillac make that kind of image transition?

Cadillac as a brand is well over 100 years old and for much of that time was the height of luxury. However, starting with the

OPEC-induced "gas crisis" of the early 1970s, GM seemed to feel the age of the brand. The cars were big, inefficient, and saddled with an old-man's-car reputation. An earlier attempt to appeal to younger drivers resulted in the Cadillac Catera, which was met by consumers with a collective yawn. And then in 2002, Cadillac launched the CTS in an attempt to go head-to-head with Lexus and Mercedes.

Compare the CTS to the Caddy of yore. It has a stiffer suspension. It has plenty of horsepower (nothing new there) coupled with a five-speed manual transmission. Putting a manual transmission in a Caddy might once have called forth cries of "Heresy!" But it was so well received that the company introduced a six-speed transmission for the 2006 model year.

Personality transplants are hard because they run strongly against the grain of existing corporate culture. Nonetheless, if carried out successfully, they can result in an infusion of new customers and energy. Take a look at your business and see if you need to act and be perceived differently.

Personality transplants have been particularly prevalent in recent years in the transportation industry. Transportation uses fuel, which causes pollution, which brings bad publicity to firms in the airline and car rental industries. To counter this, those companies are attempting to go green and become a part of the solution.

Hertz has introduced the Hertz Green Collection of fuel-efficient, environmentally friendly cars, which get over twenty-eight miles per gallon. You can reserve them online, just as you would a regular compact or full-sized car.

Delta Airlines now offers the option of carbon-neutral flights. By paying extra for your ticket you can pay to have trees planted or to build windmills, which balance out the carbon emissions you create from your flight.

Corporate personality transplants don't always work, and trying to change your brand with just a slogan can be dangerous. Remember the Oldsmobile campaign, "Not Your Father's Oldsmobile"? Oldsmobile didn't say what its cars were; the company just said what they weren't. And the campaign insulted their few remaining loyal buyers by suggesting owners of previous Oldsmobile models were old fashioned. Failure of the campaign contributed to the closing of the division at a cost to GM of $1 billion.

Solutions Group (Existing Customers / New Assets)

A relatively low-risk approach to renewal is to extend new solutions to a known base of customers. These customers already like you and do business with you. If you have a credible value proposition, there is a good chance your customers will at least test your new offerings.

But you must apply these strategies with caution. Your clients may like you, but this may only be relevant for a certain area of specialty. By trying to sell beyond this area you might dilute your positioning in their minds and appear to be claiming to do everything for everybody.

For many years Booz Allen specialized in U.S. government consulting work. When the company tried to branch out into commercial consulting, new clients said, "Aren't you the government guys?" And old clients said, "Are you taking your eye off the government ball?" To get around this issue Booz Allen split itself into two separate businesses (one focused on government business, the other on commercial management consulting) in 2008.

The following table summarizes the three Solutions strategies.

How Can We Renew Our Business?	Description	Topics to Consider
Build Share of Wallet	Meet more of your customer's needs and desires.	You only receive a portion of your customers' total purchases. Where else do your customers spend their money, and how can you win some of this business?
Shift to the Sweet Spot	Look at the value chain and develop offerings in the most attractive parts of the chain.	Your position in the value chain may have become stale and unprofitable. Who makes money in your industry, and which activities are most highly rewarded? How can you move to where the money is being made?
Leverage Your Core Competencies	Identify your core competencies and use these strengths to serve your customers in new ways.	Are your core competencies and your total portfolio of competencies underused? Start with what you do well that is valued by the customer, hard to duplicate, and can be used in many ways. Craft your offerings and then introduce them to your existing customer base.

STRATEGY 7: BUILD SHARE OF WALLET

CASE STUDY Quick! Can you name the tool and die shop that made a bid to take over the Opel car line from General Motors? The answer is Magna International. Theirs is a fascinating study of going after more and more share of wallet as a supplier to the automotive industry. Let's take a quick trip through some of their history.

1957—Multimatic Tool & Die is founded.

1960—They get an order from a car company for sun visor brackets.

1970—They expand into stamped and electro-mechanical components for the auto industry.

1973—They become Magna International.

1979—They move into automotive plastics.

1988—They move into engine and transmission components.

1989—They introduce child seats that come built into the frame of a car's normal back seat.

1994—They move into interior and exterior systems integration.

1998—They have complete vehicle assembly capabilities.

2001—They announce total vehicle engineering capabilities.

2009—They announce a takeover bid for Opel.

Although Magna International took some side-trips into aerospace and electronics, the company has found a thick wallet in the automotive industry and has found ways to make money while satisfying more and more of its customers' needs.

Your customers have more needs and wants than you are presently satisfying. What are they and what do you have to do to satisfy them and reposition your business?

Amazon started as on online bookseller. The company built an amazing system to categorize and track what its individual customers ordered so it could suggest other titles of interest. Once it had its customers hooked on the look and feel of its service, Amazon began expanding into other categories of interest to its customers such as music, electronics, and apparel.

Rather than do all of the work itself Amazon partners with other companies to warehouse and deliver its products. But everything is sold through Amazon's website, which now is close to being a one-stop shop for virtually all of its customers' needs.

Companies can go too far in search of this strategy. Starbucks started out with premium coffeehouses. Then it added snacks, CDs, books, and other nonessential items that cluttered the counters and made its stores less inviting. In 2009 Starbucks kicked off a major effort to get back to its roots. In this case, trying to sell more resulted in selling less.

STRATEGY 8: SHIFT TO THE SWEET SPOT

Sweet spots often emerge at the intersection of technology and human skill, especially when the technology supplants a human skill that takes a long time to develop. Consider the following.

CASE STUDY In the early 1970s, a Russian doctor treated a boy who had fallen and cut his eye. Curiously enough, after surgery the lad was less near sighted. The doctor hypothesized that "shaving" the eye could change its shape and, as a result, the quality of vision. This evolved into radial keratotomy (RK), a surgical procedure wherein a surgeon uses a very small diamond-blade knife to make four to eight radial incisions around the edge of the cornea. These slits make a pattern that resembles the spokes of wheel. The cuts flatten out as the cornea heals, effectively refocusing the eye and improving visual acuity.

About the same time as the development of the RK procedure IBM was developing excimer laser technology to etch computer chips. Eximer lasers produce a brief, intense pulse and can "write" with a very fine line. In 1988 IBM's excimer laser and the RK procedure came together when an American doctor performed the first laser-assisted in-situ keratomileusis. The procedure became known by the acronym LASIK and has been the sweet spot for eye surgeons ever since.

RK is very precise surgery that can only be done by highly trained ophthalmologists. Lasik surgery must also be performed by an ophthalmologist, but it is carried out by a computer-controlled machine tool that does not shake or tremble. The Lasik equipment enables a mass production approach to eye surgery, which both speeds up and limits the costs of the procedure.

Throughout the 1990s and into the current decade, as more and more people had Lasik surgery the positive word of mouth brought in more patients. More patients meant higher equipment use and, consequently, lower per-unit costs. As costs came down, prices came down. As prices came down, affordability went up.

Not sure if Lasik is the sweet spot in eye surgery? Open the Yellow Pages in any large city and look at the many pages of Lasik eye centers.

Many other companies have, in their mature phase, found a new sweet spot from which to generate profits. For example, IBM has historically been considered a computer manufacturing company. But margins and profits moved away from hardware and into software and services. To meet the changing industry IBM decided to follow them.

Today IBM makes much more money providing services to businesses than it does selling hardware. Many of its physical assets, and the people who ran them, have been replaced with knowledge assets. But for the most part, the company is working with customers they have known for decades.

In cellular phones, manufacturing is a commodity business. The sweet spot in this industry is owned by Qualcomm. It started as a contract research and development service for other firms. From there it moved to developing and patenting technology for its own benefit.

Today Qualcomm gets paid royalties by any firm using the standard Code Division Multiple Access (CDMA) technology in a phone. With more than 400 patents to protect its interests, royalty revenues approaching a billion dollars, and operating margins above 80 percent, this is a sweet spot indeed!

STRATEGY 9: LEVERAGE YOUR CORE COMPETENCIES

CASE STUDY In January 1984, Apple Computer changed the world of desktop computing. That's when it introduced the Macintosh, a small computer with a *graphical user interface*, (GUI, pronounced *gooey*). Why did this revolutionize the computing world? Because it made the computer easier to use.

Up until then you had to learn the DOS or CP/M computer languages if you wanted to perform even the simplest of tasks on a computer. Apple took us to a place where we could "point and click" with a mouse (also popularized by the release of the Macintosh) and actually get something done.

Apple (no longer Apple *Computer*) is an interesting example of a business that has exploited the true meaning of "core competency." What is a core competency, and why is it such an important aspect of renewal? Think of a core competency as a specific factor that a business sees as central to the way it works. This factor must pass three tests:

1. It has to provide more benefits to the customer than competing offerings.
2. It can't be easy for competitors to copy.

3. It must be able to be used in many different ways across many different types of opportunities.

Think about your Macintosh, your iPod, your iPod Touch, or your iPhone. What is Apple's core competency? It's the ability to make these devices attractive and easy to use. Apple studies how customers use its equipment, and then it makes the interface work just like its users think.

Does this provide customer benefit? Yes. Is it easy for competitors to imitate? No. Does Apple leverage it across all of their products? Yes again.

These days, many other companies are seeking to do what Apple did, tap into their core competencies and spread them in other directions.

Wal-Mart has been leveraging its core competencies of supply chain and buying power by expansion into groceries. The company was able to enter the food category (with devastating results for its competitors) because it already had the retail presence and the knowledge and systems for maximizing buying power. Groceries were just one more way Wal-Mart realized value from the competency it had already built.

Devon Bank started in a primarily Jewish neighborhood in Chicago. The bank built a competency in relating to and serving populations with special religious or cultural needs. But over time the neighborhood around the bank transitioned from being primarily Jewish to being largely Islamic. In an odd twist of fate, Devon Bank is now offering specially structured loans to enable its devout Islamic customers to buy homes. These loans are Shariah compliant and fit both U.S. and Islamic laws.

Transformation Group (New Customers / New Assets)

This is the most extreme form of renewal but may be the necessary choice for those businesses that are already in steep decline. Before trying any of the three Transformation strategies, however, make sure that none of the less extreme strategies will do the job.

How Can We Renew Our Business	Description	Topics to Consider
Declare Victory and Move On	Realize the value you have created and use it to create something new and different in another industry.	Perhaps you have fulfilled your dream and are looking for new challenges. Or perhaps you just want to try something new. What would you do if you had the cash and the freedom to invest it in any way you chose?
Keep the Knowledge, Switch the Business	Leverage the strength of your processes and systems to enter unrelated lines of business.	You may have developed assets/capabilities/expertise in your current lines of business that are so strong they can be used in entirely different and unrelated ways. How can you keep your core business healthy while at the same time leveraging your knowledge to enter other businesses?

How Can We Renew Our Business	Description	Topics to Consider
Cash Out and Double Down	Sell some of your business units so you can invest in, and focus on the one or more that have the most promise of success.	After scanning your portfolio it may be clear that parts of your business offer more value than others. But in order to take full advantage of these opportunities you need more scale and investment than you possess. What parts of your business can you sell to provide you with the funding you need for the stars in your portfolio?

STRATEGY 10: DECLARE VICTORY AND MOVE ON

CASE STUDY The venture capital industry is founded on the concept of declaring victory and moving on. And Kleiner Perkins Caufield & Byers (KPCB) has been among the most successful of all Silicon Valley venture firms.

In many ways, what drives venture capital firms is almost exactly the opposite of what drives other companies. When you run a company, you want it to survive and grow. For that reason, risk mitigation is always important. Venture capitalists, however, want their investments to either grow wildly so they can make a profitable exit or die quickly before much has been invested in them.

For many companies, selling off an asset is seen as an admission of failure, since it implies the company's leadership could not make the unit consistently profitable. However, venture capital's whole business model is predicated on making profitable exits. Venture capitalists like KPCB see exits (whether in the form of IPOs or acquisitions) as the big wins in their business. Success to them means getting an investment to the point that they can remove it from their books and receive the payout.

KPCB had great success with some of its early investments in the Internet, including Amazon, Netscape, and Google. In biotech they invested in Genentech. In technology they invested in Compaq, Segway, and Sun Microsystems. They invested, helped the companies grow, and then sold them off to other firms or took them public.

If you are going to truly declare victory and move on, you can't keep doing the same thing once its time has passed. KPCB is now turning away from the Internet space and funding what they believe will be the big wins for tomorrow. They have created a $100 million iFund in partnership with Apple to fund iPhone application development. Other current KPCB initiatives include Pandemic Preparedness and BioDefense, Greentech, and Life Sciences.

Declare Victory and Move On is a strategy that is employed by individuals, as well. What does a professional athlete do once his career ends at the age of thirty-five or so? He can continue to hang around his sport as a coach or administrator, or he can use his money to start something completely different.

Roger Penske was named *Sports Illustrated*'s Sports Car Driver of the Year in 1962. After retiring from racing he founded the Penske Corporation and entered the auto sales and leasing business. Today Penske Corporation is the second-largest publicly traded auto dealership group in the United States. And in 2009 Penske showed its bold growth ambitions when it attempted to acquire Saturn from GM.

However, not all second careers are a success. Football Hall of Famers Ronnie Lott and Joe Montana created the investment company HRJ Capital, which attracted investment from other sports stars. After a period of fast growth they ended up deeply in debt and were taken over by Capital Dynamics, a Swiss private equity group.

Few people in the history of business have achieved Bill Gates's level of success. After he retired in his early fifties with a personal fortune of $50 billion he focused his efforts on the Bill and Melinda Gates Foundation. The foundation's efforts to cure malaria and other diseases affecting poor people worldwide will save 10 million children's lives over the course of the next decade. What did you do this week?

STRATEGY 11: KEEP THE KNOWLEDGE, SWITCH THE BUSINESS

CASE STUDY Bain & Co. is a high-end strategy consulting firm formed in 1973. Through its work with clients, Bain gained tremendous experience in helping organizations win in the marketplace. Bain is so sure of its contribution that it measures itself on how its clients' stock prices compare to the market overall.

In 1984, several executives from Bain decided to use their business strategy knowledge in a different way. Rather than offer advice to clients, they formed Bain Capital to take equity positions in companies. By coming from the strategy side rather than the financial side of investing, Bain Capital believed it would have an advantage. The company would make investments, use its strategic insights to increase their value, and then sell them off to realize a substantial return.

Since Bain Capital's strength comes from its strategy consulting background rather than from deep expertise in specific industries it is able to move seamlessly from one industry to another in search of opportunities. One of the company's early investments was Staples when it had but a single store. Other investments include AMC Entertainment, Burger King, and Burlington Coat Factory.

From small beginnings Bain Capital has grown in size and capability. In 2006 it was the leading investor in the $27 billion purchase of Clear Channel, a large player in the outdoor advertising industry.

Today Bain Capital has grown to nearly $60 billion in assets under management and has offices in North America, Europe, and Asia. It has won in the investment industry by using the knowledge it built from its consulting roots.

In much the same way, other companies have leveraged their knowledge and skills to enter and, in some cases, dominate other industries.

Google, for example, has a powerful and proprietary approach to online search that has dominated the search marketplace. It currently has about a 70 percent share of all web searches. But although search was where the company started, it is not where it stopped. By adding new components to its search and information capabilities the company has successfully entered multiple businesses. Businesses like Google Maps, Google Finance, and Google News attract new customers and require new inputs (e.g., satellite data for Google Earth), but they all leverage the knowledge Google already possessed. Google used its powerful knowledge capabilities to switch into these new businesses while at the same time keeping their core business strong.

The Zingerman's Community of Businesses is a family of food-related businesses headquartered in Ann Arbor, Michigan. Along with their mail-order business, the company has bakery, catering, and delicatessen businesses, and it has grown to more than 450 employees with revenues of more than $30 million.

One of Zingerman's great internal strengths is its training. In fact it is so strong that it turned training into a business of its own for those within and outside the food industry. ZingTrain's offerings include "Fun, Flavorful Finance," "The Art of Giving Great Service," and "MerchandiZing!" The training business diversifies the Zingerman portfolio while making money at the same time.

STRATEGY 12: CASH OUT AND DOUBLE DOWN

CASE STUDY In 2004 Boise Cascade had a portfolio of assets few would envy. The company owned over 2.3 million acres of timberlands in the United States—property that was coming under increasing environmental and regulatory pressures.

Boise Cascade owned five pulp and paper mills and associated assets and was a solid player in the paper industry. But that industry was suffering from chronic overcapacity, and demand was projected to decline at 1–2 percent per year. Worse yet, Boise Cascade was not the dominant player in the industry. Growth was hard to find, margins were eroding, and every indication was that business conditions would continue to deteriorate as the remaining players clawed for share in a shrinking market.

The firm also owned a building products division with manufacturing and distribution facilities in the U.S., Canada, and Brazil. But it did not enjoy a dominant geographic share, and virtually all of its products were also being produced and sold by multiple competitors.

Finally, the company owned Boise Office Solutions, a leading business-to-business office supply company. But Boise Office Solutions had virtually no brand recognition among consumers, since it had no retail presence. Even more important, Boise Office Solutions was at a significant buying-power disadvantage compared to the much larger retail players such as Staples and Office Depot. And in distribution businesses such as office products, buying power is the most important success factor.

What could the company do? Most of its business units were in late stages of maturity or had begun to decline. All the low-hanging operational improvement fruit had long ago been plucked. There is always opportunity for additional continuous improvement, but that alone would not revitalize the market positions of Boise Cascade's businesses.

So in 2004 Boise Cascade sold 100 percent of their timberland, pulp and paper, and building products assets for approximately $3.7 billion. With the proceeds they purchased OfficeMax.

Combining OfficeMax with Boise Office Solutions brought the company closer to buying-power parity with Staples and Office Depot. It
also provided the brand recognition and retail presence that Boise
Cascade could not afford to build on its own. And the move shifted
its asset holdings to office products, an industry with a brighter
future than paper and building products.

Like the other U.S. Big-Three automakers, Ford had numerous brands. Some performed well, and others did not. As Ford's
leaders looked to cut costs and strengthen their brands they
realized they did not have the funds they needed to build all of
the company's brands into powerhouses. After evaluating their
portfolio, they came to the conclusion that only Ford, Lincoln,
Mercury, and Volvo had opportunities for a successful future if
they were invested in and managed properly.

To raise the money to build these brands, Ford needed to sell
off the brands that weren't going to be the drivers of its future
success. So, in March of 2008, Ford sold Jaguar and Land Rover
for $2.3 billion to the Indian firm Tata Motors.

GM followed almost exactly the same strategy in its bail-
out/bankruptcy by selling Hummer and phasing out the older
Pontiac brand. And in 2005, American Express spun off its
financial advisory group and renamed it Ameriprise. By doing
so, American Express freed itself to focus on its core credit
card business.

Selling part of your business is typically interpreted to
mean that you couldn't find a way to make it work. But, in
fact, selling off less-attractive parts of a company is fundamental to being able to properly invest funds and management time and attention into those businesses that hold the
most promise.

Applying the Twelve Strategies to Your Situation

To determine which renewal strategy is most appropriate, analyze why your business is no longer connecting to the market as it once was. It won't help you to renew your customer base if you have the wrong assets to serve them, and there's no point in optimizing your asset base if your real problem is a lack of connection to a paying customer base.

Companies whose businesses are underperforming often become introspective and focused on cost cutting in an effort to realize the accompanying efficiencies. However, it's at this time that the leaders need to look *externally*. You can deliver products and services with all the care and quality in the world; but if nobody wants to buy your products, the business dies.

There wasn't anything wrong with the VCR equipment companies were making ten years ago. The problem is that their old customers now are recording shows in digital format and storing them on hard drives. The customers have moved on, and they are not coming back.

There may still be plenty of consumers who want your product, but you might no longer deliver it in a form they want. Look at the older hotels in Las Vegas. Sure, you could gamble at one of these older casinos. But most people don't want to because these places are no longer as compelling as the newer, larger casinos. Their assets have become so outdated they are worth more as a hole in the ground for future development than they are worth as ongoing businesses.

Or consider the future of printed Yellow Pages. Boomers may love it, but Gen-Y sees no use for it. Younger consumers still need access to the *knowledge* contained in the Yellow Pages, but they are meeting these needs online and through their cell phones. Sometimes we complain that customers are a fickle lot, but the truth of the matter is that they want what they want.

Spend some time thinking about the opportunities presented by your customer relationships and the assets at your disposal. Then consider each of the twelve strategies as a possible answer for your business.

You'll find many of the answers don't fit you—they just don't feel right. But others will make more sense.

In the next chapter we will provide an overview of the process of renewal. Subsequent chapters will explain the tools and techniques that will lead you up to your own, real-world solutions.

CHAPTER TWO

The Renewal Process

The leader of every renewal effort has two objectives. First, to identify a great strategy that adds real value and promise for the future. Second, to align the organization behind that strategy and obtain the commitment necessary to make it happen. These twin objectives are not always met.

Why is it difficult to identify a great strategy that will add significant value to your organization? We see four reasons.

1. Your people are already overloaded just to run your business. Who will do the work required for renewal, and how will they free up their time to get it done?
2. The world is a complex place, and nothing about the future is certain. Because of this, you will never be able to prove conclusively which renewal alternative is the best. Your renewal choice requires judgment, and it is your judgment that will be tested.
3. Your renewal objectives may be unclear. If you don't know what you are trying to maximize and what you are willing to

trade off, it will be impossible to find an optimum solution. Without a defined set of objectives, renewal efforts tend to wander and are slow to reach closure.

4. An alternative may meet some objectives and do poorly on others. So when choosing a strategy you must eventually face trade-offs between the things you want. These are never easy.

Without a great strategy people will be unwilling to commit to a plan that appears to them to be unlikely to succeed or that appears to have limited value even if it does succeed.

Assuming you have developed a great strategy, what stands in the way of getting your colleagues to agree on it and commit to it? First, players may have different objectives, priorities, beliefs, and constraints. A particular action may be important for one part of the organization but may be a low priority for others. You need to work cross-functionally across team and business lines to successfully renew a business. And you must do so knowing that not everyone wants the same thing or sees things in the same way.

Second, some executives may be focused on organizational issues, power, and politics rather than value creation. Though everyone talks about value, many managers optimize their part of the organization at the expense of the whole.

Third, intelligent, well-intentioned people may disagree as to the best course of action. While some may have decided on what they believe to be the best strategy, others may disagree and be hesitant to commit. Others may focus strongly on a different path.

Without agreement, well-intentioned people will pull the organization in different directions. Without commitment to action, nothing will happen. The talk may be there, but the action will not be.

To overcome these hurdles, you need an effective and efficient renewal process to guide your efforts and the dialogue between the decision makers and the workers. We will cover both the process and the dialogue in this chapter.

The Phases of Renewal

The process of renewal is quite straightforward and orderly. But because renewal is not a natural event in most organizations, we have designed a process to guide companies possessing limited renewal experience.

There are three phases in the renewal process: Rethink, Reinvent, and Reposition.

Rethink is deciding which businesses need renewal and which should continue operations as usual.

Reinvent is the creation of the new business model that will provide an attractive future for the business.

Reposition is the action of transitioning from the old business model to the new one.

Each of the three phases is separated by a resource allocation decision. Between Rethink and Reinvent you must decide whether or not you are going to commit the organization to a renewal effort. And between Reinvent and Reposition you must choose the best renewal alternative for your organization.

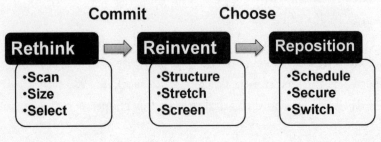

The Renewal Process

Rethink

The primary goal of this phase is to identify which parts of the business should be considered for renewal, and which should not. For those businesses that are not selected for renewal, you should continue operations under the umbrella of continuous improvement.

Rethink consists of three parts: Scan, Size, and Select. In *Scan* you examine the outlook for your portfolio of offerings and quickly identify those that do not need renewal. By removing them from consideration you are able to focus more clearly on the remaining renewal candidates. Scan focuses on the trends that are changing customers and industries and looks forward as opposed to detailing exactly where you have been historically.

Size places ballpark renewal values on each of the remaining parts of the portfolio. These will not be exact numbers. But even a back-of-the-envelope valuation will begin to identify potential opportunities for renewing parts of the business.

Select takes this a step further and identifies the short list of potential renewal candidates. It takes into account the ballpark valuation you have done, but it also factors in the probability of success, the difficulty of renewing the business, and the urgency of the call to action for the business.

We'll discuss the details of this phase in Chapter 3.

Committing to the Reinvention Effort

Before moving to the next phase, Reinvent, you must pass a key milestone. You must choose whether or not to invest the organization's top talent and resources in a renewal effort.

The short list you've compiled by Scanning, Sizing, and Selecting in Rethink is the starting point, but there is an enormous difference between having a list of possibilities and the reality of committing key decision makers and workers to the process of renewal. Some of the questions you must address before committing to a renewal process include:

- How does the priority of this renewal effort compare to the priorities of other ongoing initiatives?
- Who needs to be involved to make this a success and what is the cost of freeing up their time?
- What else is happening on the corporate calendar—is now a good time for this effort, or would it best be done later?

We'll cover the details of this choice in Chapter 4.

Reinvent

Reinvent is the second phase in the renewal process. Here's where you do the heavy lifting, looking at both what *could* be done with the business and what *should* be done with it. Up to this point you have decided which parts of your business you are going to renew. Now you have to figure out how you're going to renew them. Like Rethink, Reinvent has three parts: Structure, Stretch, and Screen.

Before you dive into reinventing your business you must be clear on the ground rules for the effort. *Structure* sets these ground rules and includes answers to such questions as:

- What would success look like?
- Who will be involved?
- How much of their time will be spent on the effort?
- What is included in the scope, and what is excluded?
- What assumptions are we making?

Structure will be covered fully in Chapter 5.

Stretch is where the team considers and puts alternatives for renewal strategies on the table. Because organizations are designed to deliver what they promise, most alternatives are not particularly audacious. But renewal demands bold choices. After all, if the mild alternatives you have been using to improve the business were doing the trick you would not be in the middle of a renewal effort!

To determine which of the twelve renewal strategies are appropriate for your business you'll need to *screen* them. If you selected the "Catch the New Wave" strategy, for example, you must decide how well it is aligned with what your business needs. What actions would you take if you were to select this strategy? How would you tailor this strategy to fit your needs?

Screen continues down the list of twelve strategies until each has been evaluated against the needs of the business. Some will fit very well, some will be close enough to be interesting, and others will be obvious nonstarters. Chapter 6 provides the detail needed to screen the twelve strategies.

Choosing the Best Renewal Alternative

Once you have a short list of attractive renewal alternatives, it is time to choose the best one for your business. This will commit you to a course that will take a significant investment of time and money, and that may take years to play out in the marketplace.

How will this decision be made? Who will make it? How will you avoid watering down the decision when trying to bring everyone on board? You must answer these questions before you choose your renewal path.

Making this choice requires evaluating all of the attributes of your alternatives. Certainly you will need to consider financial risk and return. But there are many other attributes you might also consider. What will it do for your strategic positioning against competitors? How will it affect your relationship with your customers? What are the short- and long-term implications of each alternative?

This topic is discussed fully in Chapter 7.

Reposition

The third and final phase in the renewal process is Reposition. This is the phase in which you make the transition from your current business model to the new business model.

Like the other two phases, Reposition includes three parts: Schedule, Secure, and Switch. *Schedule* lays out the tasks that need to happen in order to execute the transition to the new strategy. You will define milestones with associated due dates, accountabilities, authorities, and responsibilities, and also the sequencing of the tasks and their interrelationships.

Secure ensures you have allocated resources and that the right people have their time committed to successfully execute the strategy.

Switch makes the transition from the old business model to the new. In particular, this is where you manage the period in which both the legacy and the new business are in existence. The legacy business will be wound down while the new business is ramped up. Clearly guiding this transition is critical for successfully executing your renewal strategy.

How to handle *Reposition* will be covered in Chapter 8.

Here is a summary of the renewal process:

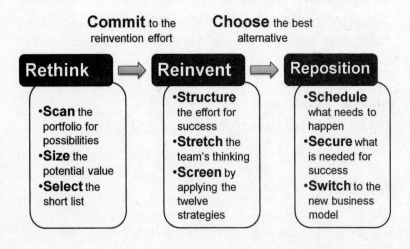

Summary of the Renewal Process

Ensuring Effective Dialogue Between Decision Makers and the Working Team

The best process in the world won't help if the dialogue between the decision makers and the working team is poor.

There are four keys to success for achieving an effective dialogue between decision makers and those charged with analyzing and executing the decisions.

- Avoid the evil of consensus.
- Minimize the arrows you shoot.
- Use inquiry rather than advocacy.
- Treat renewal as a project, not a process.

AVOID THE EVIL OF CONSENSUS

Many organizations use a consensus approach to decision making. For something as important as business renewal, doesn't consensus sound like an attractive way to go? After all, you will be working together to execute the renewal plan.

And for many day-to-day decisions, consensus works just fine. Everyone is familiar with the situation, the issues, and the range of choices, so reaching consensus is not difficult.

But for a step as momentous as business renewal, consensus is not only ineffective, it is evil. Consensus harms organizations by preventing them from solving the difficult challenges they face. It holds a company hostage to its least visionary, least creative, and most cautious person. And it forces endless unproductive meetings with too many attendees trying to forge an agreement.

Consensus also harms the relationships between individuals and groups within an organization. Under consensus people silently blame each other for holding the organization back. Since few organizations are culturally strong at dealing with interpersonal conflict, dislike and resentment will fester and be reinforced from one decision to the next.

During major changes like business renewal, leaders must do what is right rather than what is easy. It is in these actions that leaders earn their rewards, the respect of their peers, and the pure satisfaction that comes from having done an important job with excellence.

MINIMIZE THE ARROWS YOU SHOOT

How does a review of a working team's recommendations normally proceed? The spokesperson makes the presentation. Then the arrows begin to fly. "Why did you assume revenue growth of 4 percent per year?" "Why did you assume our competitors won't be able to match our price?" "Why are you asking for a 15 percent increase in marketing spending over the coming year?"

The purpose of these questions is to identify weaknesses or errors in judgment in the analysis, insight, and recommendations of the working team. You tell yourself that you're not trying to be malicious. Rather, you're confirming that a professional job was done by your workers.

But what are the unintended consequences of shooting arrows? Teams are trained to present only what they can defend. They define success as making it through the meeting without being hit by an arrow. And since it is hard enough to arrow-proof a single alternative, working teams seldom bring forward a wide range of options for discussion with the decision makers.

Operating data is an excellent tool for dodging arrows, so workers tend to present alternatives that are similar to what the organization is doing today. After all, that's where the data are most readily available.

Another unintended consequence of the arrow shooting process is to stretch out the team's schedule. Since they believe they must be able to answer any arrow shot their way, working teams go overboard in gathering information and running analyses. They do enough work to defend their decision, which is often much more than is necessary to come to a strong, reasoned decision for renewal.

Is there ever a good time to shoot arrows? Yes—after you've made a decision and once the execution plan is complete. When a team claims it has all of the answers, then shooting arrows is entirely fair and effective to see if the *i*'s have been dotted and all of the *t*'s crossed. It is when arrows are shot earlier on that we get the problems described above. Clearly, decision makers need to ask questions before approving a plan—but they need to ask the right kinds of questions. We'll discuss what those questions are in the following section.

USE INQUIRY RATHER THAN ADVOCACY

Sometimes the working team creates a recommendation and then builds a case for why it is right. They see their job as selling their recommendation to you, rather than critically thinking and evaluating the possibilities. There is a universal but sad truth—smart people, once they think they know the answer, become dumb people. They stop listening, stop learning, and stop thinking.

Once they become associated with a recommendation, people drive it through the system. They advocate for their preferred course of action and stop searching for a better choice.

The inquiry approach, on the other hand, focuses on building insights into how decision makers and workers, through cooperation, can maximize value. Inquiry sessions are not passive meetings in which the workers present and the decision makers lean back and critique. Rather, these sessions consist of engaged—and sometimes heated—dialogue between the groups as they take on the difficult issues together. Inquiry places the focus on discussion rather than on presentation.

Questions are an integral part of both the inquiry and advocacy approaches, but the type of questions you ask a working team will help turn advocacy into inquiry. If you force a team to defend a particular assumption, you will close down the discussion. Inquiry questions, on the other hand, open up the dialogue and focus both the working team and decision makers on identifying additional value. Inquiry questions stretch the thinking of the group, both on the upside and on the downside.

Here are examples of arrow questions and inquiry questions:

Arrow Questions	Inquiry Questions
Why did you assume 4 percent growth in revenues in the next three years?	How fast could revenue grow, and how could we take advantage of a fast-growth scenario?
Why did you assume our competitors won't be able to match our price?	What trends are driving the market price, and where do we stand in comparison to others in the industry and to potential new entrants?

Arrow Questions	Inquiry Questions
Why are you asking for a 15 percent increase in marketing spending over the coming year?	What should our marketing approach be to best connect with our target customers? What is the range of investments we could make to do this?

Arrows lead to low-quality conversations. The working team can probably mount a pretty good case as to why they assumed a 4 percent revenue growth rate. But they could probably just as easily justify a growth rate of 3 percent or 5 percent. On the other hand, if you ask inquiry questions, you'll open everyone's thinking and focus the discussion on how you can identify and realize additional value.

With the inquiry approach you have much more opportunity to guide and shape the thinking and the tasks assigned to the working team. You will be more active and involved with your working teams, and can make it clear to the working team exactly what you want from them.

Treat Renewal as a Project, Not a Process

Projects have a start, middle, and an end. They have timelines, milestones, deliverables, and defined roles, responsibilities, and accountabilities. Processes on the other hand, continue forever. When does accounting end? When does marketing end? The answer is that they don't.

If you treat a renewal effort as a process, it will go on and on. There will always be more questions to ask, more information to gather, and more work to do.

The renewal of your business must stay focused, move forward, and push toward a defined end. Because renewal is so important, you must have an appropriate timetable and level of resources so that the project can be successfully completed. If during the project you feel there is a compelling reason to revise the timetable, do so, but only after weighing the costs and benefits of delay.

Now that we've explained the broad outlines of how renewal happens, it's time to get to the specifics. In the next chapter we will dig into the Rethink phase.

PART I

RE**THINK**

RE**INVENT**

RE**POSITION**

CHAPTER THREE

Developing a Short List of Renewal Candidates

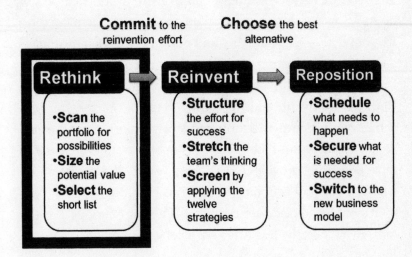

The deliverable from the Rethink phase is a short list of high-potential renewal candidates. There are three steps to reach this goal:

1. **Scan** the portfolio for possibilities: the idea here is to quickly identify which parts of the business would benefit from renewal and which would not.
2. **Size** the potential value: It only makes sense to renew if the payback for doing so is significant
3. **Select** the short list: Narrow down your possible candidates to a short list of highly attractive and realistic renewal candidates.

In Chapter 1 we suggested you consider renewal in the context of your customers as well as your assets. Doesn't it seem obvious that business leaders should constantly strive to align their offerings with the wants and needs of their customers? And yet, we can see businesses all over the world that do not do so. Why? It is not for a lack of talent or caring. In most cases it's simply that they are busy and don't notice their customers are gradually migrating away from their offerings.

Chapter 2 identified the three major phases of renewal—Rethink, Reinvent, and Reposition. The first of these is concerned with identifying those parts of your company that are good candidates for renewal. This chapter describes Rethink in more detail and provides tools to help you see the strategic gaps between you and your target customers.

It's hard to replace assets and update your offerings. But the longer you wait, the less attractive will be the remaining choices. In May 2008, a *BusinessWeek* article asked whether GM had waited too long to get serious about green. If that's the case (and we agree that it was), then by waiting too long, GM put itself in a position of having to get green fast. Unfortunately for them, the recession of 2009 got in the way, and they found themselves with a portfolio of stale brands, focusing on survival, not growth. Now that they are post-bankruptcy they may have better opportunities in front of them. But wouldn't it have been better if they had started years ago as Toyota did with its Prius?

This chapter will help you look for an imbalance between your product and service offerings and the evolving priorities of your customers. More specifically, we present and answer two questions that underlie the rethinking phase of the renewal process and help you identify those business units or product lines in need of serious renewal.

1. How fast is your industry evolving?
2. Which of your businesses are at risk, and which have renewal opportunity?

How Fast Is Your Industry Evolving?

As a business manager and executive you are experienced at dealing with in-your-face problems, whether large or small. You roll up your sleeves, get to work, and after days, weeks, or months of intense activity you lean back with satisfaction at the effort you put into solving the problem.

The truth, however, is that most of us are not good at dealing with slow, evolutionary challenges. Businesses age a day at a time, and usually you are not aware of their progression along the lifecycle curve until it is too late. You keep doing what you do best, but ever so slowly your offerings become misaligned with changing customer needs.

This was less of a problem when both product and business lifecycles were long and you had time to react, but it is certainly a problem now that lifecycles are getting shorter. Time is not on your side.

Think about your home entertainment audio system. Your record player is a 125-year-old technology that has all but died except for a handful of audiophiles who love the vintage sound of scratchy vinyl. Your radio is a 100-year-old technology that is in the mature phase of its lifecycle. Your eight-track is a 1965 technology that lasted about twelve years until it died of ridicule. Your cassette deck is a 1970s technology that was superseded by CDs in the early 1980s, which, in turn, were hard hit by MP3 technology by the mid-1990s. And if you are a member of the iPod generation you are probably on your fourth version of that technology by now.

Now think of the names of the manufacturers of these audio systems. Did the oldest keep up with the changes? Are you keeping up with the evolution of your industry? If not, you are slowly becoming irrelevant.

Innovation is invigorating. Growth is exciting. But maintaining an ongoing business is exhausting. Thinking about renewing an ongoing business can be daunting, and so we put it off until it's too late. Yet, every company will face a lifecycle dilemma—what to do before it starts to decline.

Interestingly, most managers view the lifecycle as immutable. It can be stretched, they believe, but not broken. Once a business starts its decline, the good times have come to an end. But what if you look at maturity and even the start of the decline phase as an opportunity for renewal, growth, and enhanced profitability? To do that, you first need to sense the future.

YOUR MENTAL RADAR SCREEN: A SCANNING TOOL

In a way, your perception of the future is like a mental radar screen. You can see the blips that represent incoming events,

trends, or products. You can also see blips that once were important to your business move out from the center as they become
less true or less relevant. If you track these effectively, you will
have an edge on your competitors who are focused only on the
here and now.

On the radar screen shown in the figure below we have presented three concentric zones: the Reaction Zone, the Adaptation Zone, and the Anticipation Zone. Think of the Reaction
Zone as filled with blips representing things that are urgent.
These define the agenda for most of your day with meetings,
e-mails, text messages, and other routine, time-consuming
activities. Some of these are important, others are not; but you
spend a *lot* of time reacting to them.

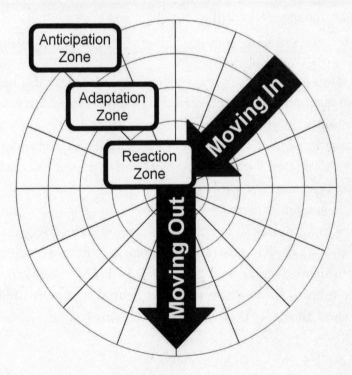

The Adaptation Zone contains blips that are farther out. They go on your to-do list but they don't require immediate action. For example, you might want to develop Spanish-language skills. Given the ethnic and linguistic characteristics of your future workforce and customer base, doing so might be quite useful for your business. After all, how can you lead when you can't communicate? But learning Spanish can wait for next week. Or next month. Or forever.

Finally, the Anticipation Zone is filled with fuzzy blips and clues about the future that are so far away you can't yet discern them clearly. Certainly they're too far away for you to take immediate action. Some of the blips are static and will never move closer. Some are coming in at an angle and will miss your Reaction Zone. But some are early warnings of major changes that will materially affect your business. How good are you at recognizing which may be important, and which are not?

Now let's consider what you should look for in these zones as you determine what parts of your business are ripe for renewal. Consider the three zones with respect to your assets and your customers' wants and needs and ask this question, "How fast is my industry evolving?" Then compare that answer to how fast your organization is evolving.

If you are evolving more quickly than your industry, you may make mistakes, but you will have time to correct them. If you are evolving more slowly than your industry, you will continually be playing catch up, but will never be able to do so. You will fall farther and farther behind your more nimble competitors.

Radar Screen Reaction Zone: What's in the Middle and Moving out Fast?

Inertia is a powerful force that pushes against Rethinking. Many things—whether processes or procedures—work the way they do because that is the way they have always worked. But in the Reaction Zone, you must formulate questions to break out of inertia, because it's here that you can most clearly see that things *don't* stay the same:

- Does your business cater to Boomers? We don't know how long this generation will continue to buy like crazy, but we do know that it's not forever. In fact, the recession of 2009 saw the Boomers begin to save at unprecedented rates. If your business is built on the assumption that Boomer spending will continue indefinitely, you may be in for an unpleasant surprise.
- Are you a Ford dealer? Where are all your buyers for mega-SUVs in a climate where gas is cheap one week and costly the next? If you've built a business on an assumption about what your customers want that is no longer valid, you need to Rethink your business model. It is in the Reaction Zone that you find out if long-standing assumptions about your business still stand.

Radar Screen Adaptation Zone: Are You Responding to the Changes You Can Already See?

Sometimes we see change coming, but we wait too long to act. The introduction of new technologies is a perennial example. It is always tempting to wait until the technology is totally ready to go. If you do so, you will lag behind those who jumped earlier.

- Are you a hospital administrator trying to decide when to switch to electronic record keeping? It certainly is the coming trend, but as of 2009 only 1.5 percent of private hospitals had electronic medical records in use across all clinical areas. The old doctors fear it; the new doctors won't practice without it. Ask yourself who will most likely still be practicing medicine in ten years.
- Are you a retailer that expects customers to walk into the showroom without having already researched pricing and features? If your business hasn't adapted to the growing sophistication of its customers, now's the time to think about business renewal.

Radar Screen Anticipation Zone: What's on the Edge and Moving in Fast?

It's hard to see the future because it seems so unformed. You can see glimpses of pieces, but not the whole. Furthermore, some of the things you see now will never become significant or may fade away. Nonetheless, to avoid being surprised you have to keep your eyes on the horizon.

- Did the local photo shop embrace digital fast enough? (For that matter, did Polaroid?) The speed of technology evolution is generally overestimated by the early adopters and underestimated by the holders of incumbent technology.
- What about the photo shop that *did* embrace digital cameras? Did they stock the software that amateur photographers might use to alter the digital photos? Did they consider adapting to consumer needs by expanding the range of products to include software and home printers?

THE LONG VIEW

The point here is that for your business to survive and not enter into an irreversible decline, you have to consider the full range of problems and opportunities facing your business. Using the mental radar screen and its zones allows you regularly to take the time to *look* for surprises.

"You want us to look for surprises?" you say.

Yes, we do. In fact, the more you allow yourself to be surprised the better you will become at seeing the future.

In the 1970s, a futurist named Joel Barker began researching what he termed "paradigm shifts"—a way of explaining how and why things change. His ability to intuit what the future held was based on his understanding of fundamental shifts in industries. These shifts often take established companies by surprise.

For example, Barker spoke of the Swiss watch industry, which prided itself on its ability to design and manufacture precision mechanical movements. The industry leaders saw the invention and development of quartz watch movements as interesting but irrelevant to their lead in mechanical design. They clung to this belief until most of the Swiss watch manufacturers had disappeared.

Our contention is that you can see clues to the future and anticipate their implications if you invest in the effort to try and do so.

Consider the digitization of medical records. You can't say with certainty when the transition will take place or what the winning technology and processes will be. But you can say with some confidence that ten years from now digitization in medicine will be the norm just as it is in virtually every other industry. You know the direction of the change, and you can evaluate how well your plans would fare as the world moves in this direction.

Start from the foundation of your business: What will your future customers want and how will you serve those needs?

Remember the classic movie *Casablanca*? A crime is committed early in the movie and the prefect of police instructs the policemen to "round up the usual suspects." We have a list of "usual suspects" to look at when you think about strategic changes to your business. Use your mental radar screen to look for the following:

Customers: Who is leaving you? Who is new? How is your customer base changing? What do your customers want that surprises you? Are customers frustrated because neither you nor your competitors can give them products and services they really want? Have you had success connecting with new customer segments?

Products and Services: Are the sales trends for your most popular products and services moving up or are they moving down? Is the competition coming out with a simpler version of your offerings? Do customers complain about the complexity of your current offerings?

People and Organization: Who is leaving your organization and why? Are most of your managers close to retirement? Do new college graduates consider your business "old"? Do you speak the language or know the customs of your newest workers, whether here or offshore? What portion of your workforce is offsite? Is that portion growing?

Resources: Are your fixed assets dedicated to one purpose or can they be used in other ways? Are your people cross-trained and up-to-date? What do you know about resources needed for the future? How will you use your knowledge of customers and suppliers to produce competitive advantage?

Location: Are you located in the "hot" part of the city, country, or world? Are you bound by ownership of land and buildings? Does your business depend on a localized customer base? Have your customers moved away from you? What is the price of labor and rent where you are located, relative to other possible locations? How competitive are your shipping costs?

Information and Communication Technology: Do you have reasonably complete and accurate information about your customers? Can your employees access the customer data they need in real-time? What do you know about your customers that your competitors do not know? What do your competitors know that you don't?

Policies and Procedures: Are you easy to do business with? What industry truths need to be challenged? (Not sure what we mean by industry truths? Go study the rise of Japanese manufacturing in the 1980s. Their ascendance came from breaking industry truths about inventory and quality, not from better assets.)

Metrics: What metrics are you using to determine the success of your product or service? Are these the same metrics used by your competitors? Are these the same metrics used by your customers? What metrics do you monitor other than financial measures of past performance?

Suppliers: How much power do they have over you? Over time are they obtaining more or less control of your business? Do your suppliers like doing business with you, or do they simply tolerate your foibles because they need your money? Are your suppliers facing economic difficulties? Is the number and quality of your potential suppliers increasing or decreasing?

Competitors: Which competitors are new to the industry? Who is considering entering that might compete in a very different way? Who is getting out of the business and why? What are competitors doing that seems foolish to you, and why might they be doing this?

Japanese Rule Breakers The ascendancy of Japanese manufacturing in the early 1980s came about by breaking two manufacturing truths about inventory and quality.

First, everyone knew that a manufacturer needed plenty of inventory on hand and people spent a lot of time and energy calculating "safety stock" levels to make sure they would not run out of needed components. The Japanese "just-in-time" inventory control concept changed all of that. Their position (heresy at the time) was that inventory should be kept to a minimum and that relationships with suppliers should be such that needed materials were delivered just in time.

Second, the industrialized nations had taken quality problems which resulted in scrap and rework as a given, and manufacturers had gone to the trouble of calculating "acceptable quality levels" for finished goods. Japanese engineers worked to get as close to zero defects as possible and made strides that major American corporations found impossible to match until years later.

Don't stop with the questions we just presented. Think about your business and develop your own set of tough questions about each of these areas of strategic change.

Renewal Risks and Opportunities

Some businesses have grown a little tired and just need some sprucing up. You see this in the local restaurant that closes for remodeling during August and opens in September with the same cuisine but with new paint, new booths, an updated menu and a warm handshake for returning customers. On the other hand, we often see businesses in need of a thorough overhaul. In the case of a restaurant that's located in a part of town that has gotten seedy, remodeling is not going to bring the customers back. The owners may need to move the restaurant and find new opportunities or go out of business forever.

What about businesses with multiple product lines or business units? What if you are Sears Holdings? Do you paint your stores to make them look nicer, or do you rethink your business model to differentiate your locations and offerings because you are in an industry with too much capacity?

Scan

What do you do after you've looked for clues about current, evolving, and potential changes? Use the following tools to start making some sense out of them. They won't give you magic answers, but they will stimulate your thinking.

- Assumption testing
- Lifecycle mapping
- GE/McKinsey Matrix
- Crafting your business model
- Evaluating your willingness to change

ASSUMPTION TESTING

All strategies are valid only so long as the assumptions on which they were built remain true. Hopefully your business was founded on a set of assumptions that have been tested and refined over time. Unfortunately, that is not always the case.

Sears Roebuck & Company built a business that thrived for nearly a century because of the assumptions they made about the habits and buying power of middle-class Americans. However, the needs of a middle-class family in the 1950s were hardly the same as they are today. Families changed, but Sears did not keep up with them. They have declined within their industry, and they may not survive unless they make dramatic changes to their business model.

Cast your mind back to when your business was started. If you have a copy of your original business plan, that's a good place to start. Look at your early marketing materials, annual reports, forecasts, and so on. These will give you a lot of insight into the assumptions which were made at the time the business began.

Now make a list of these assumptions using the following categories:

- Customers
- Products and Services
- People and Organization
- Resources
- Location
- Information and Communication Technology
- Policies and Procedures
- Metrics
- Suppliers
- Competitors

Now after each assumption, find facts and figures from your *current* financials, annual reports, forecasts, etc., that relate to each assumption. Divide them into two columns: those that support the founding assumptions and those that invalidate them.

When you've completed this part of the exercise, it should be quickly apparent to you which of your original premises for the business still hold true and which will have to be revised or discarded.

Here are some questions for you to ponder.

- *Customers:* Do you have loyal customers? Do you really know what they want?
- *Products and Services:* Do your products and services meet the evolving needs of future customers? Do they provide the best value?

- *People and Organization:* Do you have the right workforce? Does your workforce have the best leaders?
- *Resources:* Are your resources relevant? Are they effective and efficient?
- *Location:* Are you located in the best place for the customers? Are you in the best place for the workforce?
- *Information and Communication Technology:* Is your technology "user-friendly"? Is it up to date?
- *Policies and Procedures:* Are your policies and procedures convenient for your customers? In what ways do you make it hard to do business?
- *Metrics:* Are you measuring the right things?
- *Suppliers:* Do your suppliers see you as a "partner"? Have you picked suppliers based on price or on competency?
- *Competitors:* Do you know all of your competitors? Do you know what motivates your newest competitors?

When the authors conduct planning sessions with clients, we ask them two questions about their assumptions. First, we ask them if they can think of assumptions their organizations' leaders made in the past that became less true over time. Then we ask them a second question: "What assumptions are you making today about your business that will be considered foolish in five to ten years?"

LIFECYCLE MAPPING

You might think that the lifecycle chart we showed in the introduction to this book is simply a description of sales volume over time. It's that and more; it can be an analysis tool that you use to chart your position at a point in time or to chart the evolution of your business. It might seem that many established businesses are in the mature stage for a long time. However, product lines and business units can mature quickly, and you want to seek out signs of maturity in time to work on renewal.

Apple did a brilliant job with the introduction of the iPod, iPhone, and iPod touch. As of mid-2009 they had sold nearly 220 million iPods, and realized more than $38 billion in revenue. From less than 5 million units per year sold from 2002 through 2005, they ramped up sales to over 50 million units per year from 2006 through 2008.

Their sales are beginning to decline, however, and the sales curve looks like the mature portion of a lifecycle curve. The challenge to Apple's leadership, then, is to renew their business model or face continued and accelerating decline. Given the attitude of their organization toward risk taking and their excellent track record, we suspect they will succeed. A likely candidate for this renewal may be their iPad tablet computer.

As you look across your business, evaluate your assets and your customer base to see where you have the best chances of renewal success. Look at your assets and customer base as they've evolved over the lifecycle of the business. It's not enough to evaluate your customers as they are now; you have to look at how they've changed since the business started and what the customers of tomorrow will look like.

Do you have assets, either hard or soft, that are healthy and can be repurposed? Can you adapt them to new customer needs while keeping the business going? Likewise, as you examine your customer base, do you see a base that is in decline or a base that is still viable but has moved away from your existing offerings? To identify high potential renewal candidates you will need to build deep insight into customers' current and future needs *and their willingness to pay* if you satisfy those needs.

For years and years both Kodak and drug stores such as Walgreens and CVS served a population that "took pictures." Kodak manufactured film, and the drug stores provided a film distribution channel as well as a drop-off point to get the film developed. All in all, it was a very profitable business for both parties and typical of a mature business model that had run steady state for years. However, the rapid shift in technology away from film-based cameras to digital cameras has forced Kodak to dramatically renew its core business and do it quickly. Its film business is nearly dead, so it has to rely more than ever on its photo paper and kiosk-based printing equipment.

Retailers are using Kodak kiosks to bring people into their stores. Its success will depend on how well these retailers keep the kiosks up, running, and easy to use. So now Kodak's success relies relatively less on its own manufacturing quality and relatively more on the service level of its retail partners.

Kodak is facing an additional challenge from printer manufacturers that want people to print their photos at home using their ink and paper. Will we stay at home and print our photos, or will we get in the car and drive to Walgreens and use the Kodak kiosk located there? So far, retailers such as Walgreens appear to have a good sense of what their customers want and what they are willing to pay. Serving the picture-taking public may be a nice little earner for the drug stores, but it is a company-defining opportunity for Kodak's renewal.

The State of Your Industry
You must also analyze the health of your industry and the capabilities of your current and future competitors. For

example, the business traveler was the "sweet spot" for airlines for decades, and airlines competed with one another for the business flyer's business. They courted frequent flyers, and all the major airlines created "clubs" so that business travelers could have a comfortable place to wait and meet.

But air travel continues to become more of a hassle at the same time that video conferencing is taking off. Is United Airlines' future competitor American Airlines, or is it Cisco's or AT&T's teleconferencing capabilities? If it's the latter, United should think about what it offers that teleconferencing doesn't. Think back to the list of renewal strategies from Chapter 1. United's asset base is not very flexible, so it will need to find new customer opportunities to successfully renew itself.

How do you use it to determine which of your product lines or business units are candidates for renewal? Draw the life-cycle curve on a whiteboard or a large sheet of paper. Now, based on input from your sales and operations teams, plot on the curve where you feel each of your product lines and business units falls. If you're a young company, the preponderance of marks will be on the left side of the graph. However, most ongoing businesses are surprised to see many of their offerings and businesses fall into late maturity or early decline.

THE GE–MCKINSEY MATRIX

This framework was developed by General Electric in cooperation with McKinsey & Company, a business consulting firm. The matrix is a systematic approach that enables a multibusiness corporation to prioritize investments among its business units. It organizes their thinking about existing and potential businesses by looking at them from two points of view: the attractiveness of the markets in which they operate and the strength of their competitive advantage within those markets. The matrix plots these factors on two axes.

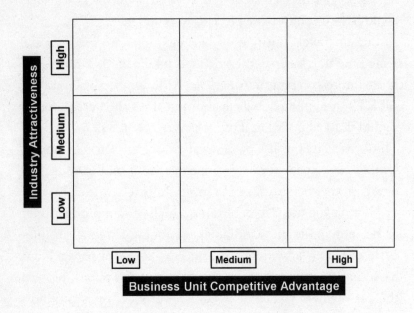

GE-McKinsey Matrix Industry Attractiveness

What makes a market attractive? Growth? Profit levels for incumbents? Attractiveness often depends on who's looking at the market just as much as it does about the market data itself. Large companies are rarely attracted to small markets unless they see the potential for rapid and substantial growth. This is the position, for example, that the big pharmaceutical companies have taken with respect to the bio-tech market. They watch it, and when it begins to grow they buy into it.

As you examine your business units from the perspective of Industry Attractiveness you will want to consider such factors as:

The size and growth potential for the product. For example, in today's technology environment is there more potential for vacuum tubes or microprocessors? It depends on who's asking the question. We doubt that Intel would see vacuum tubes as a sizable market. That said, there are small companies that are doing quite well serving this niche market.

Cyclicality and demand variations. In general, companies like a steady-state environment because it is easier to maintain profitable use of assets. However, some companies are just fine with the ups and down of demand variability because they can respond quickly (and charge for it.)

Entry barriers. All of us would love to have the field to ourselves, but that's hard to do. In the pharmaceutical or microprocessor industries, it takes billions of dollars to gear up a new plant. If you're already a leader in one of those industries, you can be assured that no new competitor will suddenly pop up. On the other hand, if you're running a nail salon, you might find a competitor has moved in next door over the course of a weekend.

Profitability and risk. Do you prefer large profits accompanied by large risk or smaller profits accompanied by lesser risk? Pharmaceutical companies often generate seemingly large profits, but they assume billions of dollars of risk every time they launch a major drug. Grocery stores have very small margins, but they provide for a need that will exist for a very long time. Assessing the ability for any player to make a profit is key to understanding the risk of moving into an industry.

Differentiation. Face it, commoditization equals low (or no) profits unless you are the low-cost player. If you cannot differentiate yourself in a meaningful way, you will be forced to do too much work for not enough reward. So consider— does the market you are considering offer the possibility of differentiating your products or services?

GE-MCKINSEY MATRIX—BUSINESS UNIT COMPETITIVE ADVANTAGE

The GE-McKinsey Matrix plots attractiveness along the vertical axis. The horizontal axis of the matrix considers your advantages or disadvantages compared to existing and potential competitors. As you examine your business units from the perspective of competitive advantage you will want to consider such factors as:

Your reputation for quality. Who has the better reputation: Nordstrom or Sears? What advantages does that give one over the other? A lesson many American manufacturers learned the hard way in the 1980s and 1990s is that a reputation for quality correlated with profitability.

The strength of your brand. Your brand has an inherent strength made up of components such as awareness, customer loyalty, satisfaction, profit trends, and geographic spread. It's an asset, and like other assets a strong brand can be a barrier to competition or an anchor holding you back. Who has the stronger brand, Twitter or the *New York Times*? The answer depends on whom you ask. Older customers love the editorial integrity of the *Times*. Younger ones prefer the speed and spontaneity of Twitter.

Loyalty. This advantage is temporary at best. Like a reputation, it takes a long time to build, but it can be lost in a very short time.

The strength of your hard and soft assets. Would you rather have in-house expertise or everything outsourced? Now that all major American manufactures of consumer electronics have offshored or gone out of business do you think that a U.S. company could still become a credible name-brand manufacturer in the coming years?

Economies of Scale. How big are you compared to the market share leader? What are the implications of your relative size on buying power, name recognition, and capability to invest?

As you consider these and other factors, place your business units where they belong on the matrix. Then step back and evaluate your company as a whole. Business units that fit into the Low-Low or High-High intersections are probably *not* good candidates for renewal. The Low-Low units should be shut down or sold. You can spend a lot of time and energy here and gain nothing. The High-Highs are wonderful and you need to put your energy into running them as best you can. Renewal can come later. It is at the intersections of Mediums and Highs where you will find those units that may benefit from renewal.

As you think about renewal or staying the course, make sure that you have not been swayed by emotional or cultural factors. We find, for example, that a unit that was "the founder's baby" is often ranked higher than it deserves on both axes.

Likewise you have to consider your true position in an industry and ask if you need to move to another market to succeed. Need an example? Consider the American food icon, McDonald's.

In the late 1990s and early years of the 2000s McDonald's acquired a significant interest in a number of related companies—Donato's Pizza, Chipotle, Boston Market, and Prêt a Manger—and it looked as if it was trying a transformation strategy—that is, it was moving away from fast food and into companies aimed at a different segment of the market.

Now McDonald's is out of all of these companies. Why? Were the industries attractive? They were probably medium to high on the Industry Attractiveness scale. What about McDonald's competitive advantage? Given the company's supply chain skills and ability to manage restaurants it had to be on the high end of the scale. So why not stick with these new brands as a strategy to renew a mature business?

Now we don't have any inside information, but it seems likely that the opportunities, although good, were too small to be material for a company the size of McDonald's and would be a distraction to a management team trying to grow a global business. McDonald's may be in a mature industry, but it has a significant opportunity to continue to grow before it hits the decline stage. It may seem mature in the United States, but it's in a growth portion of the lifecycle in China.

The lesson here is simple: Just because you *can* renew your business does not automatically mean that you *should*. Renewal is a judgment call—not a spreadsheet exercise.

Crafting Your Business Model

Your business model is the description of who your customers are, what they want from you, what you offer them, and how you produce and charge for your products and services. All companies have a business model, even if the executives, managers, or workers can't tell you what it is.

These business models must reflect the reality of where you are along the lifecycle curve. And at some point you will have to consider renewing all or part of your business. You can either make changes to your business and then figure out the impact on your business model, or you can rethink your business model and design into it the changes necessary for renewal. We think it makes sense for you to "think first."

Your business model is a blueprint of who you want as customers, what you are promising them, how you fulfill your promises, and how you will make money doing so.

TARGET CUSTOMERS

Start your thinking by asking yourself what customers you need if your business is to succeed and what customers you should avoid. Success depends on customers with real wants and needs and the money to pay for your products and services. As for avoidance, ask any professional services executive about clients that are so much bother that they would like to fire them.

Another thing to consider is whether today's customers fit the profile of the target customer you want and need in the future. In the early 2000s, American auto companies loved all their SUV and big-truck customers. Now they are fighting to find ways to make themselves relevant to buyers of smaller, fuel-efficient vehicles, customers whom they had spurned during the glory days of "bigger is better."

Today's customers are a gift not to be wasted; tomorrow's customers are a treasure to be found.

COMPLETE OFFERING

Satisfying customer needs is more than putting your product or service in front of them. It consists of four interrelated components: your value promise, your relationship, your product or service, and finally your communications.

Value Promise

Your value promise is built on a thorough understanding of the stated (and sometimes unstated) needs, wants, frustrations, and trade-offs of your target customers. Your customers will rate you on whether or not you consistently deliver on this promise.

Relationships

Why are relationships so important? The reason is tied to the issue of value promise. We buy from people we trust; we are more likely to trust people we know and who have delivered on their promises in the past.

Products and Services

A promise is meaningless unless you deliver on it. And the only real judge of the success of this delivery is the customer. Your product may do everything your engineers say it should, but it must provide the benefits that your customers expect.

Communication

Real communication is both message and feedback. So ask yourself: How do you know what your customers really expect of you?

The blogs and wikis that are at the heart of Web 2.0 can move us much further toward powerful communication capabilities. They can lead to important conversations between sellers and the buyers. Or they can be a waste of valuable time as your workforce checks in several times a day to see what their kids are up to on their Facebook pages.

COMPETENCIES AND OTHER ADVANTAGES

Renewal strategies are built on the assets at your disposal. The possession of assets is a starting point but, in the end, it's how you use them that will make a difference in the level of success your organization achieves. Entrepreneurs are often asset poor so they make maximum use out of what they have. Larger, well-established organizations are often asset rich but they sometimes squander them.

NETWORK OF ACTIVITIES WE AND OUR PARTNERS PERFORM

Look at the success of Southwest Airlines in the latter half of the twentieth century. What made them so good? Michael

Porter, the Harvard strategy guru, attributes their success to a network of activities that made them unbeatable. Their value promise was to be *the* low-cost airline, and all of their activities were aligned with that promise. ("Gee, we would love to serve food on our flights, but that wouldn't make us *the* low-cost airline.")

How do you get your products and services to your target customers? Do you go to them or do you make them come to you? Bookstores were hurt by Amazon's easy process that delivered books to consumers' homes. Physicians' practices have been affected by the availability of basic care at convenient retail clinics like CVS's MinuteClinic or Walgreens's Take Care Clinic.

Furthermore, how do your target customers want you to distribute your goods and services? Remember long ago when ATM machines were new? Many of the bank's best customers saw no need for them because they wanted to talk to a "real person." Now fast forward to today—would you even think of working with a bank that did not have a great ATM network? Customers have come to *expect* ATMs despite their previous resistance.

Often executives limit their thinking to their current, in-house capabilities. This is too narrow a point of view. All companies need suppliers, alliances, and partners of various sorts to succeed. Selecting the best partners to work with you is paramount to your success. Toyota's rise to dominance in the 1980s was built on a network of suppliers that allowed it to implement what, at that time was an earth shattering innovation—just-in-time manufacturing. That innovation changed the face of manufacturing across every industry—and

Toyota could not have done it without a dedicated network of able, willing, and dependable partners.

RULES, BELIEFS, AND NORMS

Every organization plays by a set of rules, some stated and some implicit. For example, all organizations need to bring in more revenue than they expend in costs, but the rules of "not-for-profits" and "for-profits" are different. A company run for profit *must* realize significant goals not merely for revenue but for its bottom line.

One of the biggest rules of the game guiding for-profit organizations is making their numbers for the current quarter—sometimes even at the expense of the long-term interest of the company. Executives talk about "taking the long-term view" but those words are often not put into practice.

Here are some other questions you should ask yourself about your company's rules, beliefs, and norms:

- How do you treat your employees? Do you consider them to be partners?
- What does the word "ethics" mean in your organization? How far will you stretch your principles to make a profit?
- Is the customer your number one consideration?
- What's your attitude toward risk?

The answers to these questions will determine how you conduct your business model in the real world.

Evaluating Your Willingness to Change

At this point, you must ask yourself: "Given your history, culture, market position, and business processes, can you 'make it happen'?"

Go back to the list of things you can change. Now ask if there are items and categories that have such a strong emotional or cultural tie to your organization that you will be unable (unwilling) to change them.

- *Customers:* Would you be willing to abandon your best customer?
- *Products and Services:* Is your current product or service your business identity? How much leeway will your customers give you if you choose to make a change?
- *People and Organization:* Could you leave your team behind and start over with new people? Do you have the desire and energy to build a new organization?
- *Resources:* Could you demolish your original factory?
- *Location:* Would you move to another neighborhood? Another state? Another country?
- *Information and communication technology:* Could you give up the "tried and true" for leading-edge technology?
- *Policies and procedures:* Are you willing to admit there are better ways?
- *Metrics:* How focused are you on financial results versus other important metrics of performance?
- *Suppliers:* Can you leave your oldest friend in the industry?
- *Competitors:* Are you willing to consider that there are new (and better) competitors?

Size

At this point you do not have enough knowledge to perform a defensible valuation. Instead, in Size you are making a ballpark estimate to determine if there is enough value potential to justify renewal. To size the value consider the following:

- How could renewal affect your fixed costs?
- What percent margin increase could you expect from successful renewal?
- How would renewal affect your growth rate?

For each of these we suggest testing sensitivity by using a range of inputs (low-base-high). It is often easier to reach agreement on a reasonable range than to reach agreement on a single point estimate.

Consider Apple's new iPad. It is difficult to credibly project what its sales will be three years from now. It could skyrocket, as so many other Apple products have. Or it's possible that consumers don't really need a product in between their smart phones and their laptops, and the iPad could be a dud.

A single estimate of iPad sales will almost assuredly be far off the mark. But a range will have a very good chance of including the actual sales figures. And by thinking in terms of ranges, Apple will spend more time developing contingency plans for both optimistic and pessimistic scenarios than the company would if it just assumed a single sales estimate.

Select

We have introduced a number of tools to use as you rethink the staying power of your business unit. Now take some time to consider your product lines and businesses and see if any of them are candidates for renewal.

- Use the Radar Screen to list and examine factors that you should anticipate or to which you have to adapt. Consider your present business and ask, "What's in the middle and moving out?" as well as, "What's on the edge and moving in?"

- Use assumptions testing to examine the foundation beneath your existing business strategy. Do you see any weaknesses or holes in the way you make money? Look at your current business and identify the assumptions that underlie your revenue and profit generation capabilities. Likewise decide if there are better ways to gain new customers or build new assets.

- Plot all of your product lines or business units on the life-cycle curve. Which are in late maturity? How fast are units moving to the right? Can you keep these alive with product-line extensions or easy moves into adjacent areas? If not, how much time do you have before you either renew or accept decline? Now plot these same pieces on the GE/McKinsey matrix. What is this tool trying to tell you about what to renew?

- Take a careful look at the components of your business model and see if your total offering meets or exceeds the needs of your target customers. Do you know what they really want or are you offering them what you gave them in the past?

Have their expectations drifted away from your products and services over the years? Can you fulfill your value promise and make a profit? Should you spend the money and the management effort to renew your capabilities?

The Rethink phase is the time to think big, bold thoughts and play out plenty of what-if scenarios. It's very important, but relatively stress free. You'll have plenty of time to stress when you commit to the effort to renew.

CHAPTER FOUR

Committing to the Reinvention Effort

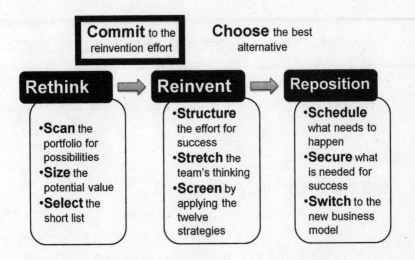

You know your renewal effort is important. But how critical is it compared to other organizational priorities? Unless your decision makers see the renewal effort as meriting their time, it will be doomed from the beginning.

At the end of the Rethink phase you identified a short list of business units that were strong renewal candidates. In this chapter we discuss how to commit the necessary resources to fund one or more reinvention efforts. In Reinvention you will be investing resources to create and evaluate renewal possibilities.

This is a major step for your company. It is easy to talk about the need for renewal, but it is much harder to make time for it in the corporate calendar. In doing so, you are choosing to invest an organization's time, attention, and resources to reinvent your approach to one or more of your products, services, or businesses. It is unlike other major decisions in several crucial ways.

- Renewal entails more risk and uncertainty than other decisions.
- Renewal raises the question of the viability of your business.
- Renewal requires different measurements than day-to-day decisions.

Risk and Uncertainty in Renewal

Organizations are designed to deliver excellence in day-to-day operations. Their measurements, rewards, systems, and procedures are designed to deal with normal operations. Predictability is central to running a mature business, but it is not even peripheral to renewing one. What works for typical operations may destroy any chance of successfully renewing your business.

Among the questions raised by renewal are:

- Will you be able to find an attractive and feasible renewal alternative?
- What are the consequences of choosing poorly?
- What will the risk and return profile look like for the renewed business?
- What is the probability you can successfully execute your renewal plan?
- How will the employees react when they hear of the renewal effort and its implications?
- What will happen if word of your plan leaks out to your customers, partners, and workforce before you are ready to communicate and execute it?

Viability of the Business

When you are running a business, you typically don't question its viability. When things get tough, people redouble their efforts and do their best to meet their targets. But they seldom address the question of whether the business has a future, and if so, what it might look like.

Committing to renewal changes that. No matter how attractive the renewed business might be, there will be members of your team who do not want to, or who are not capable of, making the transition from current operations.

When individual leaders decide to renew part of their business, they expose their careers to possible harm. For an ambitious leader with a desire to create a positive future, renewal is a career-accelerating opportunity. But for many managers, taking a chance at losing is something to be avoided rather than embraced.

Different qualities will be on display in renewal than are shown when running a business. People's creativity, imagination, boldness, and vision come to the front in renewal. These are characteristics not ordinarily prominent while running a business.

Committing to renewal effort requires a leap of faith since the alternatives that will be developed and the choice that will eventually be made are not yet known.

Renewal Requires Different Measurements

How do organizations judge the quality of their decisions? Normally, based on their outcomes. If the results you realize are better than your targets, you have done well. If they are worse, you have done poorly. This is simple and straightforward.

For a manager with hundreds or even thousands of daily decisions, this makes perfect sense. If you are making a sufficient number of similar-sized decisions, some decisions will get great results, and some will get poor results. But on average, if someone is making good decisions, she will deliver good results at the end of the year.

But what if this same approach of judging decisions by their results is applied to major decisions that do not balance out over the course of a year? Since managers are judged and rewarded based on outcomes, people will hesitate before proposing a renewal alternative that has significant risk associated with its return. And since there is no way to renew a business without taking risks, this is a problem.

Suppose, for example, a renewal alternative was being considered that had a risk and return profile as shown on the next page.

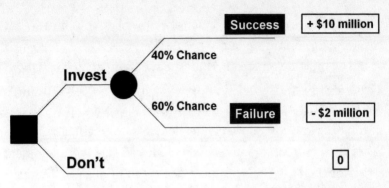

Investment with Both Risk and Return

There is a 40 percent chance to make $10 million and a 60 percent chance to lose $2 million. For the shareholders, this looks like a wonderful opportunity. The expected value (also known as the mean or the probability weighted average) is 40 percent of $10 million less 60 percent of $2 million for a total of $2.8 million. In other words, if the owners made this investment many times they would, on average, be $2.8 million better off each time than if they did not invest.

But consider the manager who has been developing this investment opportunity. How easy will it be for her to bring forward a recommendation with a 60 percent chance of failure when she is being measured and rewarded based on outcomes? After all, in this example the most likely outcome is that she will fail.

Where will the manager spend her time—trying to find ways to leverage the upside and make even more than $10 million, or finding ways to reduce the risk of losing $2 million? If she is like the vast majority of clients we have asked this question of, her focus will be on minimizing the downside.

Consider the question her bosses would probably ask her: "Suppose we make this investment and our competitors beat us to market with a better product at a lower price point. What can we do to minimize our exposure?"

Now imagine, instead, that she's talking to a far-sighted group of leaders. Rather than focus on the downside, they say, "Suppose this investment really takes off. What can we invest in today at low cost so we can triple our investment six months faster than currently planned?" These leaders are willing to take a risk for the long-term prospect of a substantial gain. Unfortunately, such leaders are a minority in today's business community.

Leaders talk about "maximizing value," but when you look at their actions they give up value on the upside in their quest for protection on the downside. Organizations don't maximize value; they minimize the number and magnitude of bad things that can happen to them.

Organizations are typically delighted when they invest and things go well. They rarely think that with some risk taking and forethought they could have created twice the value. People are rewarded and punished for the results they actually realize. They are seldom penalized for what they *could* have realized.

If you judge your people based solely on outcomes, you encourage your best talent to set aside renewal alternatives that carry risk and promise substantial returns. Instead employees will clean up last year's plan and come in with modest improvements that will probably work to some extent but that will not be sufficient to renew your business.

If this is to change, you need a new way of thinking about large decisions like renewal. You must be able to discuss the quality of these decisions *before* you make them.

But how do you judge the quality of a decision before you make it? You do so by applying the seven attributes of a high-quality decision.

The Seven Attributes of a High-Quality Decision

To obtain full commitment to a renewal effort, you need to build quality into seven attributes:

- Objectives
- Structuring
- People, Culture, and Decision Process
- Choices
- Knowledge
- Evaluation
- Execution

OBJECTIVES

Objectives asks and answers the question, "Who are the players, and what do they want?" Players are those who will feel the impact of the decision. They might include customers/clients, joint venture partners, shareholders, the executive committee, division management, and the workforce.

For example, one of us worked on a relatively simple issue of deciding on a hospital location. The client had already selected a city and had narrowed the choice down to two locations, which they referred to as A and B. The client had studied this topic six times and still couldn't choose between the two sites.

We asked, "Who are the players, and what do they want?" It turned out the crucial players were the physicians who ran the organization, and what they wanted was a short commute. Location B was cheaper, but Location A was closer to the fancy neighborhoods in which the physicians lived. The first six analyses recommended B because that was more cost effective than

A. But cost was not the only objective of this decision. By not focusing on the key players and their wants, and by neglecting to analyze commute patterns at rush hour, the working team missed a crucial trade-off.

STRUCTURING

Structuring answers questions such as:

- Where does this effort fit within the organization's priorities?
- At which level in the organization should this decision be made?
- Who should make the decision?
- What assumptions are reasonable?
- Which topics will be included in this effort, and which will be held until later?
- How much time and resources will we invest in this renewal effort?

As an example, consider the launch of a new product by the Singapore office of the Asian subsidiary of a U.S.–based company. At what level should this launch be decided? At the Singapore level, since they have the relevant expertise and are closest to the market? At the Asian subsidiary level, since funding will come out of the overall Asia budget? At the corporate level, since the product launch will affect the overall brand? Structuring defines the decision, and therefore specifies to a large extent what the end product will look like and how the work will get done.

The danger of poor structuring is that you make a decision, but it doesn't stick. Singapore rolls out its product, and

Corporate steps in because they see risks to their brand that were not considered when the decision was made at lower levels.

PEOPLE, CULTURE, AND THE DECISION PROCESS

Do you have the right people involved to make the decision? Do you have the appropriate people involved in analysis and information gathering? Do they have sufficient time allocated to do what needs to be done?

A critical success factor for decision making is pushing authority down to the right level in the organization. When a company is first created, most of the critical decisions can be made by a small number of people at the top. In maturity, its complexity prevents a small group from making all of the decisions. If the organization survives, it is because it has learned to push decision making down in the hierarchy.

Decision makers and the workers need to engage in dialogue. The decision makers need to hear how their workers think so they can decide how much weight to give the working team's recommendation. The workers need to understand how the decision makers think so they can build their own perspective and strengthen their decision-making capabilities.

CHOICES

Choices describes the full range of potentially winning alternatives open to your organization. The purpose of developing choices is not to find the single perfect path—you will never be able to do so. Instead the intent is to stretch your organization's thinking and ensure potentially valuable ideas get on the table.

The search for choices should not be superficial. If any of your choices are obvious losers, you must remove them from consideration.

Consider the set of choices developed by a small offset printing company in Minneapolis. Their industry had been turned upside down by the transition to digital printing. They responded by identifying several possible paths. They could continue to offer a full range of printing services. Or they could choose to deliver some of these services themselves and partner for others.

Another alternative was to become a printing broker. Rather than do the printing themselves, they could rent unused capacity from firms that had already invested in the latest and most efficient presses. Another alternative was to move toward the creative side and focus on developing the concept and detailed design.

Or they could shift to a customer-service focus and work with clients to develop the concept and then delight them with service upon completion of the job. Then again, they could merge with one of the new, state-of-the-art digital printing firms. This would combine their design and customer service strengths with the digital capabilities they themselves could not afford to build.

In the end they chose to merge with the digital printing firm. This enabled them to enter the new generation of printing. Their competitors, which could not make this leap, have gone out of business one after the other.

KNOWLEDGE

Knowledge in the context of renewal decisions is not about what you know but about what you *don't* know. For example, you know the estimate for next year's revenues. It is listed in your planning documents. But you don't know what next year's revenue is really going to be. It might turn out to be much higher or much lower than the number on which you are planning.

Decision making is all about the future. But there are no facts about the future. Study though you might you will never know for sure what will happen until it does. That is why you should approach uncertainties as ranges, not as point estimates.

When you think of uncertainties, consider the following:

- Which people in your organization have the best expertise to provide estimates on the key uncertainties?
- Do they have the latest historical data and analyses to inform their assessments?
- Are they biased either for or against the opportunity in a way that might lead to an improper assessment?

Take for example the problems with subprime housing lending in 2006–2008. One of the authors worked with a major mortgage-backed security player in 2005. The professionals in this firm were flying high and making money hand over fist. They were convinced the good times would keep on rolling.

Then the subprime crisis hit. Housing prices softened then dropped. Default rates went up. Refinancing became much more difficult. And the mortgage-backed security business transformed within twenty-four months from the land of milk and honey to a world of unending pain.

Could the mortgage brokers have predicted the change in the market with certainty? Of course not. But they had been assuming the future was going to be like the present or the recent past. Had the leaders of the mortgage-backed security firm thought more about the range of possible future scenarios, they could have taken precautions and shortened their road to recovery.

EVALUATION

Evaluation deals with the question, "How do each of the things we can do (our choices) rate against each of the things we want (our objectives)?"

Some of these ratings will be quantitative. For example, if you are looking to build a hospital at location A or location B you will create a spreadsheet to quantify your cost estimates. However, some important ratings may be qualitative. Physicians' attitude toward a commute from their home to location A or to location B may be hard to quantify. You certainly could estimate the average commute time in minutes. But what about the overall commuting experience, which includes the scenery and the frustration caused by traffic? These may be even more important than the commute time, but again they would be difficult to quantify. Proper evaluation requires you include everything that is important, whether you can quantify it or not.

EXECUTION

A decision is an irrevocable allocation of resources. Until you have committed people's time and attention and the organization's financial resources, you have not decided. If you make a decision, and then make it again when capital budgeting time comes around, you never really made it the first time.

The questions to ask about execution include:

- What does the execution timeline look like, and what are the key deliverables along the way?
- Who will lead the execution effort? How much of their time will be spent on this effort, and how will their time be made available?
- Do they have the funds they need to successfully execute the selected alternative?
- Does everyone involved with the execution effort understand what was actually decided?

Once you have answered these questions you are ready to shift from the decision-making project to the execution project. As Peter Drucker said, "No decision has been made unless carrying it out in specific steps has become someone's work assignment and responsibility."

Applying the Seven Attributes

The quality of a decision is limited by whichever of the seven attributes is the weakest for that particular decision. For example, if Knowledge is weak, even if the other six attributes are strong, your decision will be poor. As the saying goes, garbage in, garbage out. What if Objectives are weak? Your decision will leave out important criteria and is likely to be second guessed.

To make sure that your decision is as good as it can be, do the following exercise. On a large piece of paper, list the seven attributes we've discussed. Now get red, yellow, and green markers.

If you're confident that you've answered each of the questions attached to an attribute and you feel good about the answers, circle it with green. You're good to proceed. If you've only answered some of the questions or you're not sure about your answers, circle it with yellow. And if you have little confidence that you have either the right questions or the right answers, circle it with red. Red means you are not ready to go yet, and you need to do more work.

Here is how the decision makers rated the quality of the hospital example (Location A or Location B) over the four meetings between the decision makers and the workers:

	Meeting 1	Meeting 2	Meeting 3	Meeting 4
Objectives	Yellow	Green	Green	Green
Structuring	Green	Green	Green	Green
Choices	Red	Yellow	Green	Green
Knowledge	Red	Yellow	Yellow	Green
Evaluation	Red	Red	Yellow	Green
Execution	Red	Yellow	Green	Green
People, Culture, & Decision process	Green	Green	Green	Green

Red-Yellow-Green Ranking of the Seven Attributes

Take a look at the column under Meeting 1. Is this a good place or a bad place to be after the first meeting? Overall, it is pretty good. Yes, you still have reds. But at this stage you have not defined your choices or gathered your knowledge. How could you have possibly completed a credible evaluation?

The attributes aren't separate; rather, they interact with each other. For example, once you understand commute time to the hospital is an important objective for the physicians, you will gather knowledge on commute times. You might also create new choices that include a parking garage to reduce uncertainty in the physicians' daily commutes.

Three attributes should be addressed before the others. They are: Objectives, Structuring, and People, Culture, and the Decision Process. Objectives come early because you need to start with the end in mind so you know what you are trying to maximize. Structuring comes early because you need to define the decision and how you are going to go about making it. And People, Culture, and the Decision Process comes early because unless you get the right people involved you will not be able to go to green in the other attributes.

The red-yellow-green approach improves decision making by focusing your effort on improving those attributes that are limiting the quality of your decision. It lets the decision makers and the working team know what is left to do before a decision can be made with confidence. The work of a decision maker is this: Move the reds to yellows, the yellows to greens, and avoid wasting time fine tuning those things that are already green.

Finally, and perhaps most importantly, the dialogue that occurs when decision makers and working team members discuss the ratings improves everyone's insight into the decisions.

Decision-Quality Diagnostics for Renewal Decisions

Consider a reinvention decision you are facing today. To decide whether or not to, use the chart below to rate each of the attributes red, yellow, or green. If you have great answers to the two questions, you are green. If you have okay answers, you are yellow. And if you have few credible answers to the questions, you are red.

Objectives	• How much risk can you take with this business in both the short- and long-terms? • What are the key objectives with respect to renewal for each of the key players?
Structuring	• Which parts of the business are in need of renewal, and which should continue on their current path? • Where does renewal of this business fit within your organization's priorities?
People, Culture, and the Decision Process	• Who would the decision makers be for a renewal effort, and are they committed to investing their time to renew this business? • Who is required to do the work of renewal?
Choices	• What choices are you faced with if you do not commit to a renewal effort? • Which strategies should you be considering for renewal?
Knowledge	• What are your key knowledge gaps? • Do you know enough about potential customers, offerings, and competencies to be confident in your choice of strategy?

Evaluation	• What is the potential financial value of successfully renewing the business?
	• Which nonfinancial values should be included in your evaluation of the alternatives?
Execution	• Are you prepared to allocate the resources necessary for a renewal effort?
	• What capability gaps must be filled to successfully execute the renewal effort?

PART II

RE
THINK

INVENT

POSITION

CHAPTER FIVE

Structuring Your Reinvention Phase

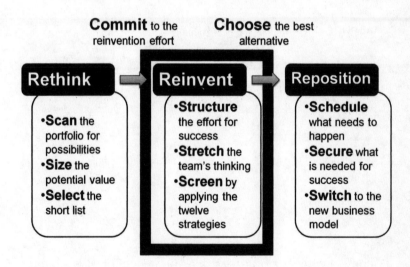

Now that you have determined which (if any) of your business units are ripe for renewal, you can move to the next phase of the process. In the *Reinvent* phase, you will develop the strategy for renewal that best meets your company's needs.

This phase has three parts:

1. **Structure**, in which you'll get the various pieces of your organization ready to launch the renewal effort.
2. **Stretch**, in which you'll prepare your team members to think broadly about the task before them.
3. **Screen**, in which you'll decide which renewal strategies of the twelve we've outlined should be serious contenders for your final strategy selection.

Structure

Structuring has eight pieces. They are:

- Leadership
- Confidentiality
- Objectives
- Mission Statement
- Assumptions
- Phases
- Timing
- Connection

These eight sections will take up much of this chapter. Too often people jump into renewal before clearly thinking it through. But that road leads to failure. Rather than pay heavily down the road, it is better to take time upfront to set up the effort for success.

Leadership

Renewal initiatives need a sponsor with enough organizational clout to enable the working team to do its job. You may fill this role or, depending where you are in the power hierarchy, you may have to find a sponsor. The important point here is that the sponsor must possess the necessary authority to make decisions about renewal—both strategically and tactically.

The role of the sponsor includes chartering the effort, defining the decision makers and the working team, and assigning the project leader. It is the sponsor's responsibility to get the right people on board.

The sponsor also makes the necessary resources available to the team. In addition, the sponsor may be called on to run interference for the team with high-level management and also be called on to remove any roadblocks as they arise.

A strong project leader ensures the working team will stay focused and on schedule. She will identify issues and develop plans for addressing them in partnership with the project sponsor. It's essential that her leadership of the renewal effort be seen as a dedicated assignment with sufficient time set aside to do the work properly. It cannot simply be piled on top of an already full workload.

Once the project leader has been selected, it is time to fill out the working team. For an effective working team you need representation from the different parts of the company that will be affected by the decision. At the same time, the working team should be small enough to get things done.

CONFIDENTIALITY

Confidentiality is necessary in renewal since you will be planning major changes to the business. The last thing you want is for word to get out that you are considering closing an office or plant. Such things can be a considerable distraction to your organization and customers.

Be clear on the following points:

- Who needs to know there is a renewal effort underway?
- Who needs to know the intermediate results and insights along the way?
- Which parts of the renewal plan can be shared fully with the company, and which parts should remain confidential?

OBJECTIVES

You must define your objectives in the renewal effort at the very beginning. Typically objectives encompass such things as:

- Growth and profitability targets that will make the renewed business a valued part of the overall portfolio.
- Growth and profitability targets for the legacy business during the transition.
- Maximum allowable risk in the renewal effort.
- Competitive positioning after the renewal effort.

MISSION STATEMENT

The mission of the effort is defined by answering three questions: What are we doing? Why are we doing it? How will we know if we succeed? If you don't know the answers, don't start your renewal efforts.

You might also consider a fourth question: How could we fail? By answering this question you can identify potential stumbling blocks before you hit them.

Once you've answered these questions, embody the answers in a paragraph that sets forth the mission of renewal. This mission statement will remind your people why they are doing this effort and will help keep the entire team focused and on track.

ASSUMPTIONS

The purpose of stating your assumptions is to identify possible conflicts or differences of opinion early in the process. Try to identify up front the difficult issues and sources of conflict that must be dealt with to successfully renew your business.

For example, you could assume that "we are going to maximize value." That is true, but not everyone may agree on what this means. One decision maker may think it means you need to acquire a regional competitor. Another may think you need to add services. A third may think you need to slash staff to get your costs in line.

To properly define your assumptions, you must establish three things:

- What will you assume at the start of the effort?
- Which decisions will you make during the effort?
- Which decisions will you hold until later?

Assumptions can be both useful and dangerous. They are useful in that they enable you to more closely define the scope of the work you're doing. They are dangerous in that they can lead you into bad decisions should your assumptions be faulty.

For example, suppose you took it as given that you should only look inside your current region for new opportunities. But if you have already mined that area thoroughly, there may be little opportunity remaining. Because of your assumption, you will not look at other regions and may miss significant chances to grow.

PHASES

Divide your renewal effort into phases, each of which is manageable and lasts no more than three to four months. Phases may be completed more quickly than that, but anything longer tends to wander and lose focus. If you try to do everything at once, it's like trying to boil the ocean—you may put in a lot of energy, but not much happens.

For example, phase one might include a decision on which geographic markets your renewed business should target. In phase two you might decide where to locate your office, how to staff up with local personnel, and how to introduce your products and services to the local business community.

Just because some decisions must be held until later does not mean they are unimportant. They may be huge investments that are critically important to the organization's success. But they should trail today's decisions as opposed to lead or be made in parallel with them.

TIMING

Setting up the timeline and the required resources is key to a successful renewal effort. Rather than treating renewal as an ongoing process (in which case, it will continue forever), you need to treat it as a project, one that has a beginning, a middle, and a measurable end. At each stage, set milestones:

- When do you need to finish the effort?
- To meet that date, when do you need a completed evaluation?
- To meet that date, when do you need your choices defined and your knowledge gaps filled?

CONNECTION

A major challenge in renewal is connecting the decision makers and the working team early and often. Set up a short discussion session between the decision makers and the working team at the close of each of the working team's sessions. Doing so takes the focus away from preparing formal presentations and places it on an engaged conversation between the decision makers and the workers.

Stretch

Stretching your thinking is fundamental to renewal efforts. You already know a lot about running your business and about the opportunities adjacent to your current operations. If you are going to succeed in your renewal efforts it will be because you stretch your own and your team's thinking beyond what you have done in the past.

Begin the stretch process by reviewing and/or completing the strategic analysis you developed in *Rethink*. At this point, you should know the answers to questions such as these:

- Where are the emerging needs of our existing customers?
- What new customers are potentially interesting to us, and what would be attractive to them?
- How do we compare to the strongest competitors in these areas of interest?
- What new types of competitors might enter with different capabilities?
- Where are the greatest opportunities for increased value?
- What are the critical success factors for winning in these opportunities?
- How well positioned are we with our people, competencies, and systems to take advantage of these opportunities?
- What skill and knowledge gaps must be filled to set us up for success?

DEVELOP POWERFUL AND DISTINCTIVE CHOICES

How effective are you at putting strong choices on the table and giving them serious consideration? For maximum effectiveness, your alternatives must be both creative and feasible. The different choices must span the range of possibility and stretch your thinking beyond what is provable or defensible. Equally, alternatives must build off your competencies, be affordable, and have clear roles, responsibilities, and accountabilities.

Organizations are generally not designed for creativity. They are built to deliver excellence in day-to-day operations. True creativity tends to reduce productivity in the short term as new approaches are tested and either succeed or fail. Anything new and different will take time today, though it may benefit you tomorrow. Because of this, creativity all too often gives way to expediency.

When Fred Smith was a student at Yale, he submitted a paper outlining his idea for an overnight package delivery company. The professor graded it a "C" and wrote, "The concept is interesting and well formed, but in order to be better than a 'C', the idea must be feasible." Smith went on to found Federal Express. It takes brilliance to create a great idea, but anyone can shoot holes in it while it is in its early stages of development.

Renewal requires creativity. You need a structure that forces you and your team to search for value. Applying a renewal strategy forces your team to stretch. By considering which is the right strategy, team members will be forced to think outside their comfort zones.

Screen

Suppose you needed a new suit. What would you do? You would go to your favorite retailer and try a few on. Hopefully you could find one that fits you well enough that you could wear it with a few minor alterations. We have developed twelve renewal strategies organized into four different groups. Your job is to try on each of the twelve and find the ones that fit you the best. You will keep the best and screen out the rest.

In order to do so, ask yourself these questions:

- Could this strategy revitalize our business and provide us with our targeted level of growth and profitability?
- What level of competitive advantage would this strategy deliver?
- How challenging would it be to successfully execute this strategy?
- What is the risk involved in this strategy?

Try each strategy, test the fit, and then move on to the next strategy. This screening process will result in a short list of strategies that closely match your needs.

Certain characteristics are associated with the successful implementation of each of these strategies. The more of these characteristics you have (or the more you can build or acquire) the better the match will be between your situation and that strategy. In the *Choose* phase you will narrow your short list of possible strategies to the single alternative that will become your renewal strategy.

The characteristics of each strategy are described in detail in the next chapter.

CHAPTER SIX

Coming to Grips with the Twelve Renewal Strategies

Your business serves a portion of your customers' needs, and their needs are, in turn, a portion of the total available market. That, in turn, is a piece of the overall economy. It's a given that changes have occurred and will occur in each of these realms. Your job is to keep your business relevant and profitable in the midst of this change.

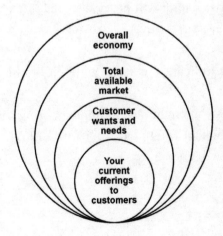

The Context for Renewal

We've Been Down This Road Before

The bad news is that you have to renew your ongoing business. The good news is that others have done so before you, and you can learn from their successes and failures.

Although every business is unique, each has to maintain alignment between what their customers want and the products and services they offer to meet those needs.

You might renew your business by adjusting your offerings to fit the wants and needs of your existing customers. Likewise, you might build on your existing knowledge of your customers and see what else they need and where they spend their money. Or you might look to the total available market and extend your business to satisfy the needs and wants of new customers. Finally, given your understanding of the condition of your business and the condition of the marketplaces, you might want to stretch yourself and take advantage of other opportunities afforded by the general economy.

In Chapter 1 we presented a brief overview of the twelve strategies. This chapter will provide some "thought starters" as you consider each of them.

- **Clues** that indicate this strategy might be the right one for you.
- **Challenges** you might face in implementing this strategy.
- **Assumptions** for you to examine and confirm.
- **Risks** you will encounter.

New Concept Group (Existing Customers / Existing Assets)

Renewal Strategy 1: Catch the New Wave

You use this strategy when you shift your current business to the next "hot thing." You might lead the way or, more likely, you might look at your market and see where new offerings are emerging and old offerings are becoming obsolete.

CASE STUDY In the first six generations of the video game home console market Nintendo was not the standout manufacturer. Nintendo's sixth generation GameCube sold more than 20 million units, but that was less than a fifth of the units sold by the market leader, Sony's PlayStation 2.

During the first six generations, video game console makers competed on price and computing power. Each new generation had more processing power, more memory, and more realistic graphics than the last. They competed on the ability of the box to create more and more realism in the play of video games.

Then in 2006 Nintendo launched the Wii just in time for the Christmas buying season. The graphics of the Wii weren't an advance. In fact, if anything they were a step back. They looked cartoonish compared to the photorealism other consoles were producing. But the Wii experience was totally different from anything that had been seen before in the play of video games.

Before the Wii, video game players sat side by side, staring at the television while their fingers flew on their hand-held controllers. The players had little direct interaction with each other and made almost no physical movement.

Gaming is different with the Wii. Games are played standing up, and players direct the action by moving their body and the controller. Instead of paddles, buttons, and joysticks, an accelerometer inside the controller senses movement and uses that to control the game's action.

The demographics of the Wii are unlike any other gaming console. Wii bowling tournaments with eighty-year-old participants are held daily at rehab centers across the country. Standing and moving is what these seniors need to regain their strength and range of motion after an operation or illness.

The Wii is a social experience. Players don't focus on the Wii itself while they are playing. Instead the Wii creates an impromptu party with excitement and energy coming from the interactions of the participants as they play the game.

The Wii created a new wave in console video games. Over 50 million Wii consoles have been sold, about the same as the combined total of seventh-generation Xbox360s and PlayStations.

CLUES

If your sales are lagging and you're losing customers, you may be missing something new that has entered the marketplace. It's best if you already have people looking for "the next new thing." Some companies hire futurists; others identify some of their trendier employees as "cool hunters." Ask yourself what new products or services you're seeing in your industry. You may be seeing clues to industry change.

CHALLENGES

The major challenge in using this strategy is to differentiate between a fad, which may be profitable in the short term but unsustainable in the long term, and a real trend. A second challenge may arise if your leadership team feels out of its comfort zone. They may see the new trend but deny it because it makes them uncomfortable. Most shoe companies, for example, missed the "Crocs" phenomenon.

ASSUMPTIONS

This strategy depends on you being in tune with your customers. Some "old line" companies, unfortunately, seem to think they know more about needs and wants than their customers do. Kodak missed the digital photography wave by assuming that most camera users would hold on to their trusty 35mm cameras for more years than they did.

It is dangerous to assume that even if you start off behind the trend, you can always catch up. That may have been true for much of the twentieth century, but it is less valid in the twenty-first century. Product lifecycles have gotten shorter and shorter. Consumer electronics companies that are chasing the iPod are after a very fast competitor. By the time they catch up to the current incarnation of the iPod, it will be old news. Apple will have moved on to newer and greater offerings.

RISKS

The biggest risk associated with this strategy is that you may get the timing wrong. For some businesses this is an inconvenience; for others it a major problem. For example, in the 1990s many hospitals assumed that as Boomers aged they would need more open-heart surgeries. To prepare for this, hospitals went through a long process to build and equip surgical suites and recovery areas. In doing so they missed both the wave of new drugs that reduced the incidence of heart attacks and the use of stents, which keep clogged arteries open. Both of these reduced the demand for heart surgeries, and many hospitals were left with expensive underused assets.

Renewal Strategy 2: Put Old Wine in New Bottles

Use this strategy when you see the need to repackage or rebrand your offerings. You sense that your offerings are no longer exciting and, therefore, you are in danger of losing your best customers. Your offerings may still fulfill your customers' needs but they need to seem "fresher."

CASE STUDY Kentucky Fried Chicken was founded in 1952 by Colonel Harland Sanders. He built the business on the back of his "finger-licking good" secret recipe of eleven herbs and spices. Herbs and spices still sound good today, but how about the term *fried*?

In today's health-conscious world no firm wants to highlight that their food is deep-fried. Any firm that did would feel out of touch with today's consumer. *Fried* is old wine indeed.

In 1991, Kentucky Fried Chicken changed its name to KFC. The company changed its logos and signage and dropped *fried* from its name entirely. The change worked for many years. Young people have good awareness of KFC but are surprised to find the initials stand for anything.

Then, a bit surprisingly, in 2007 KFC brought back its old name and signage. Kentucky Fried Chicken returned, but now it had shifted focus. Rather than avoiding the word *fried*, the chain touts its healthfulness. KFC was among the first of the fast food chains to shift to trans-fat-free oil. They now use soybean oil to cook all of their fried offerings.

In 2009, KFC continued their health push with the introduction of "Kentucky Grilled Chicken." The grilled chicken is marinated in the secret recipe before being grilled. To help position this as a healthy product, KFC hired the number-one-ranked women's beach volleyball team of Elaine Youngs and Nicole Branagh to be their spokespeople. You can't get much healthier than beach volleyball.

When it comes to old wine, KFC seems to have a large inventory of new bottles.

CLUES

The biggest clue lies in the words customers or suppliers or employees use to describe your business and its offerings; if they refer to your services or products as old, stodgy, dated, or musty, you should consider this strategy as a possible solution.

CHALLENGES

Real rebranding is difficult to accomplish. It means more than changing the words your ad agency uses. The "new bottle" we speak of has to be meaningful, not just cosmetic.

McDonald's "I'm lovin it" campaign did a brilliant job of presenting a mature, U.S.–based company in a new way. This campaign was McDonald's first global advertising effort. And it was more than just words to consumers. Crews worked on ways to treat customers in a "happier" manner. Menu changes focused on mothers, giving them a reason to bring their kids into the restaurant. And the quality of coffee was upgraded around the world.

At the same time, the *fundamentals* of McDonald's didn't change. The company maintained its focus on providing an instant meal to its customers, one that can be eaten in the restaurant or taken away.

ASSUMPTIONS

This strategy assumes you are in tune with your customers and that you know what they want, not just what they have bought in the past. A second assumption is that the new package or the new look will resonate with your customer base. A third is that the increased value resulting from the change will outweigh the confusion or inconvenience the rebranding creates among your customers.

RISKS

You may change your appearance to the point where you alienate your best customers. That won't be all bad if you can replace them with new customers. Philip Morris accepted this risk and succeeded in the 1950s when they purposely shifted Marlboro cigarettes from a female- to a male-targeted brand.

Marlboro was originally released as a women's cigarette (that is, filtered) when it was launched in 1924. However, after World War II the potential for real growth was with male smokers. In 1954, Leo Burnett (the man, not the agency) launched the "Marlboro Man" ad campaign focused on getting male smokers to switch to filtered cigarettes. Marlboro succeeded, and versions of the campaign ran until recently. Marlboro was willing to lose its female customer base because it expected—rightly—to replace them with male smokers.

On the other hand, if you undertake this rebranding and fail, you may lose your identity and confuse not only your best existing customers but the entire available market as well. Remember the "New Coke" fiasco?

Another example of failed rebranding: In the late 1990s, the city of Las Vegas attempted to move away from its Sin City image and promote itself as a capital of family-friendly entertainment. The city tried to hide or at least gloss over the gambling, drinking, and sexual freedom that had been a part of Las Vegas since its founding. On the whole, the campaign was a failure; families with small children did not come to the city in large numbers, and the idea of a family-friendly Vegas discouraged those in search of an adult-oriented playground. The result was that in 2002, the Las Vegas tourism board promoted a new slogan: "What happens in Vegas stays in Vegas." Sin City returned to what it does best.

Renewal Strategy 3: Revise Your Profit Model

Value migrates, and so do profits. That's the point of the book, *Value Migration*, which Adrian Slywotzky published in 1995. For example, in the early years of the personal computer revolution, companies assumed that the big profits would be in assembling and selling hardware. However, starting in the 1980s, Microsoft proved that much larger profits lay in creating and selling the software that powered computers. The result was that Microsoft rapidly outstripped IBM and other manufacturers in profitability.

Likewise, profits migrated from those companies that designed personal computers in the early years of the PC era to those that designed microprocessors. Consumers saw the value in the chip, not the box. Consequently, Intel enjoys profits that might have gone to IBM and the PC clone-makers because of their brilliant marketing campaign—*Intel Inside*.

If, in your marketplace, you see that profits in another sector are outstripping yours, you have the option to renew your business by revising your profit model. If you don't, you will have to accept commodity prices and lower profits.

CASE STUDY Movie making is a high-risk proposition. Total costs for an effects-filled summer film can approach $200 million. Should a film turn out to be a blockbuster, the returns can be enormous. The three *Lord of the Rings* movies cost New Line Cinema an average of $100 million each and grossed nearly $3 billion in the worldwide box office. On the other hand, a flop like Warner Brothers' *The Adventures of Pluto Nash* cost $100 million and returned one tenth that in ticket sales.

To revise their profit model, studios have changed the way they compensate their stars. They hire the same actors but pay them in a way that reduces the studios' risk.

Traditionally actors were paid a fixed fee (running between $10 million and $20 million for top talent) for each film. The actors received their payments whether the film was a blockbuster or a disaster. All of the risk on the downside and opportunity on the upside was retained by the studio. Now, however, studios offer actors smaller fixed fees up front and provide contingent payments depending on the film's success.

The biggest stars get "first dollar" payments. In other words, they start getting their contingent payments with the first ticket sold. More common are back-end contingent payments, which only kick in once the picture has broken even.

The effect of this payment structure is to transfer box office uncertainty from the studios to the stars. If a film flops, the studio feels less pain because it pays less to the actors. On the other hand, if the movie does well, the studios do not realize as high a return because the actors' payout grows.

An extreme example was Warner Brothers' deal with Jim Carrey in 2008 for *Yes Man*. They gave Carrey no upfront payments at all. Instead he received 36 percent of the gross once the film had recouped all of its costs. Had the movie bombed, Warner Brother's would have saved the $20 million or so Carrey would have demanded as a signing fee. As it was, the film was a huge success at the box office, and Carrey may have earned double his usual fee.

By revising their profit model the studios have reduced the uncertainty in their movie investments. Using this new profit model also enables studios to negotiate deals that would be too expensive if they had to guarantee payment for everything up front. In the end a studio may pay more for a star, but only if the company itself is making good money from a movie.

CLUES

Look for decreasing margins and decreasing revenue. Decreasing margins suggest that your current offering is becoming a commodity, insufficiently differentiated from similar products. If your revenue and/or volume are decreasing, this might indicate you are losing business to competitors with a different value proposition. Be on the lookout for companies that charge differently than you do.

Verizon Wireless, faced with extensive competition in the wireless market, differentiates itself by offering not only monthly plans, but also prepaid cell phones. Customers pay up front for a phone that has a set amount of minutes already programmed into it. When the initial prepaid minutes run out, customers can buy additional minutes. This enables Verizon to offer phone service while giving customers various payment options.

CHALLENGES

The biggest challenge is timing the shift. If a pharmaceutical company waits for its patented drug to go off-patent, it almost always loses to a manufacturer of generic drugs. If the pharmaceutical company produces its own generic version of the drug while still on-patent, it loses some revenue but maintains better control of future revenue streams. The challenge is figuring out when to make the shift from branded to generic. If they move too soon, they will lose considerable revenue. If they wait too long, they will face head-to-head competition from generic drug manufacturers who have lower cost structures and can beat them on price.

ASSUMPTIONS

Revising your profit model assumes you understand the costs associated with each product line and each business unit. Take a look at how you allocate your overhead costs. Do you spread them across all business units, or do you allocate them based on the activities needed to support each business unit?

RISKS

If you stay with the status quo too long, you may miss the opportunity to shift your profit model. The major music companies fought digital downloads to the very end in their effort to sell bundled "albums." In doing so they alienated both their customers and many of their artists.

On the other hand, if you move too soon, you may leave profits on the table. Nearly all newspapers offered free news in their early response to the Internet. But once customers became accustomed to getting the news for free they resisted paying for a subscription to an online version of the daily newspaper.

Extension Group (New Customers / Existing Assets)

Renewal Strategy 4: Aim Higher or Lower

This strategy is built on your ability to move significantly up market or down market to serve customers you previously could not reach. Marriott has decided to do both—going up market with J.W. Marriott Hotels and Resorts and down market with their Springhill Suites and Fairfield Inn properties.

CASE STUDY Samsung Electronics ranked sixteenth in *BusinessWeek*'s listing of the fifty most innovative companies for 2009. This is not at all surprising, given the buying power of the younger cell phone and consumer electronics users of today. It is, however, an interesting story of business renewal.

Samsung was founded in 1938 and grew over the next half century to become the largest business in Korea. However, a bold move in 1977 laid the foundation for the renewal that would take place thirty years later. This bold move was the decision to engineer color televisions. In retrospect this may not seem to be such a big deal, but it had profound repercussions for the company.

From its founding until the 1970s, Samsung grew into a huge conglomerate competing in heavy equipment, sugar production, construction, and the "new" electronics industry. However, by the 1970s it was best known for mass production of commodity electronic components and consumer electronic devices. It moved into the manufacture of black-and-white televisions in 1972 and had become the largest mass producer of such sets by 1976.

In 1977, Samsung leadership decided to engineer color TVs, not just assemble them. This move to "aim higher" was especially bold because Korean television stations had not yet begun broadcasting programs in color. Samsung Electronics had to rely solely on exporting to overseas upscale markets. And here is where one seemingly small renewal strategy became the foundation for "big time" renewal.

By the late 1990s, the Samsung Group was in serious financial trouble. Other Asian manufacturers had outperformed them as advanced technology became more and more important, especially in the then-growing cell phone business. By 1998 Samsung's chairman was worried about the survival of the company.

Realizing that "commodity = low margin," Samsung focused its efforts on Samsung Electronics. They felt aiming higher provided the best opportunity to prosper in an upscale market because of the competencies they had built while engineering their televisions. To realize their vision of aiming higher, they shut down over thirty businesses and sold another forty. Since they did so, their market share and margins have grown substantially.

Their success today was built on a decision to aim higher in 1977. It is not always a single bold strategy that leads to renewal. Sometimes it is a small decision that over time sets the stage for larger decisions.

CLUES

Look beyond your existing target customers to the total market for the type of product or service you provide. Do you see basic needs that you can fulfill at a profit? Does the market seem much hotter either above or below your price point?

CHALLENGES

Your target customers may not identify with your brand and resist it in higher or lower manifestations. Wal-Mart is perfectly capable of sourcing and distributing high-end women's clothing. But that doesn't mean wealthy women will shop there.

The challenge in moving down-market is that your overhead costs may be too high for you to maintain target profit margins if you lower your prices. Nordstrom could sell inexpensive clothing, but, given the costs of their infrastructure, they couldn't make a profit doing so.

ASSUMPTIONS

The successful execution of this strategy assumes that you have the needed assets and capabilities to create products or services aimed at up-market or down-market offerings at a reasonable cost.

RISKS

The big risk with this strategy is that you may damage the reputation of your base brand if you don't pay attention to quality. Selling down-market should *not* mean that you create substandard goods or services.

Renewal Strategy 5: Make a Time Shift

As businesses embrace the global economy, executives must think in terms of a twenty-four-hour clock. However, the shift is more than altering opening and closing times. You may have to alter your products and services to fit the new times of operations. People used to complain about "bankers' hours" when they had to wait for the bank lobby to open. Now we have twenty-four-hour access to our accounts—as long as we don't mind using a computer or an ATM.

CASE STUDY What do you get when you mix breakfast cereal with nuts, pretzels, butter, garlic powder, and Worcestershire sauce? You get Chex Party Mix, a snack that is consumed in the evening hours.

Ralston Purina, originally a grain business that focused on animal feed, rethought its business in the 1930s when it had to find a use for surplus grain. It entered the breakfast cereal business and created the Chex line of cereals.

By the early 1950s it was rethinking its business again and came up with a way to get people to consume a breakfast cereal at "non-breakfast" times of the day. Fortunately, Americans had a new pastime that was "hands free" but consumed most of our evenings. We were sitting passively in front of televisions and needed (wanted) snacks.

Purina time-shifted (and increased) the consumption of its base product by adding a recipe on the cereal box for a "party mix."

Cereal was no longer something to consume only after waking up; it also became something to consume before going to sleep.

Purina sold the line to General Mills, and in 1994 that company produced Chex Mix as a stand-alone product. This is a different channel to be sure, but it's still cereal that's not tied solely to breakfast.

Sometimes you time-shift to use your assets more uniformly, while other times you get your customers to time-shift to increase consumption of your base product.

CLUES

The bluntest clues are the complaints of your customers about your hours of operation. Subtle hints are seen in the rise of entrepreneurs offering services at "off-hours." Your favorite dry cleaner may only be open from 6:00 A.M. to 7:00 P.M. But if you live in any reasonably sized city you could almost assuredly find some other dry cleaner that stays open around the clock. Check out your competition. Are they offering non-standard hours that are draining your customer base?

CHALLENGES

Although you may already possess the physical assets to operate around the clock, you probably don't have the workforce and the supervisory team to staff new hours of operation. Furthermore, you will be challenged to communicate with supervisors and workers at times that are convenient for both of you. You might find people who are willing to work the graveyard shift; are you willing to lead them? You might find a firm in China or India that can handle your call center. Do you know their culture well enough to connect with them?

ASSUMPTIONS

In addition to assuming you have the personal wherewithal to handle a twenty-four-hour operation, another big assumption is that you can keep costs in line with potential revenue and that you can ramp-up successfully. Domestically, second- and third-shift operations traditionally incur a cost premium because these shifts pay a slightly higher wage (called a shift differential) in order to attract people willing to work at night. Global operations will require travel to meet and understand the new workers. Additionally, customers will not naturally think of you off-hours, so you will need to invest in advertising and communication to spread the word.

RISKS

The major risk is that the cost of new hours of operation will exceed your revenue potential. For example, although Krispy Kreme Doughnuts has been around for over a half-century, its national expansion took place in the early years of this century. Part of the company's appeal was the twenty-four-hour operation and the freshness of the product. However, getting hot, fresh doughnuts at 2:00 A.M. meant that everything had to be up and running even when there were few customers to buy. The company's explosive growth soon tapered and off-hours customers dropped—but Krispy Kreme's costs remained high.

Renewal Strategy 6: Get a Personality Transplant

Every business has a personality. Apple has cultivated its rebel image since the early days of the Mac. On the other hand, IBM is "all about business." Southwest Airlines has a "serious but fun" attitude about it, while Singapore Airlines pampers you. Mercedes Benz is a "serious money" automobile; BMW is a "driving machine." What's the personality of your business and could you renew your business by changing its personality?

Getting a personality transplant is a bit like rebranding, but on a much more pervasive scale. The personality of your business is exhibited in the totality of all that you do and produce. It's reflected in your corporate culture. If you adopt this strategy, you will have to make a conscious decision as to who you want and do not want as customers and in your workforce.

CASE STUDY What was the largest grossing entertainment opening day ever? *Spiderman 3* at $151 million? *The Dark Knight* at $158 million? The answer is the video game *Call of Duty: Modern Warfare 2,* which sold $310 million on its first day in North America and the United Kingdom. Video games are big business, and Activision is one of today's premium developers. But that was only after the company performed a successful personality transplant.

Creating a modern video game is far too complex to be done by individuals and much too expensive to be funded by small groups. But the creativity necessary to envision and create a top-selling game is endangered by the efficiency required by large companies.

In the early 1990s, Activision was spinning its wheels because of endless arguments between creative designers and financial management. And while the staff was arguing over costs they weren't making great games.

Activision hit rock bottom in 1991. Bobby Kotick crafted a takeover of the company for $440,000 as part of a prepackaged bankruptcy. His first move was to fire 142 of Activision's 150 employees. Then he rebuilt the company from the ground up to appeal to creative game makers.

He abandoned the commoditized approach to game development and placed his bets on unleashing the creative people to do as they thought best. Along with this creative freedom came measurements and rewards based on the performance of their games franchises.

This approach has paid off handsomely:

Title	Copies Sold	Gross Revenues
Call of Duty	33 million	$1.8 billion
Tony Hawk (skating)	40 million	$1.6 billion
Guitar Hero	25 million	$2 billion
World of Warcraft	11 million	$1 billion in annual subscriptions

If your business is creativity, focusing too much effort on gaining efficiencies will lead to failure. But do you have the courage to place your bets on creativity over control? Activision did, and its personality transplant has resulted in billions of dollars in sales.

CLUES

Look at blogs and posts that your customers are writing and see what words they use to describe you. (By the way, if your company isn't being discussed in the marketplace, that in itself is a clue you are a wee bit out of touch.) Are you resonating with your future (younger) customers? If not, you may need to get a more youthful personality.

CHALLENGES

This strategy can make senior management uncomfortable. A big challenge is to get them to listen to the need for a transplant. This strategy may also require a change in company culture, one that makes everyone a bit uneasy.

ASSUMPTIONS

This strategy is built on the assumption that the senior team is listening and is willing to consider a change in personality. Likewise, you are assuming that your workforce will embrace the new personality over time. It won't happen quickly, but it must happen.

RISKS

The biggest risk is that you aren't able to convince your customers of your sincerity to change. Oldsmobile couldn't pull it off; Harley Davidson got it. Oldsmobile gave us words; Harley gave us better quality, a (respectable) "club," and a much cleaner image than the outlaw biker/Hell's Angel of the 1950s and 1960s. Another risk is that you may trip up on internal resistance. Some employees might be quite comfortable with the current personality and will be unable or unwilling to make a change.

Solutions Group (Existing Customers / New Assets)

Renewal Strategy 7: Build Share of Wallet

Even your best customers do business with other companies. How can you expand your offerings to go after these extra dollars? How can you adjust your value proposition so that you get more of your customers' total spend?

The big consulting firms are masters of this—they look for evolving problems to resolve for their clients and then find the resources to solve them. Workers in muffler shops discover they can fix brakes as long as the car is up on the lift. Chiropractors offer acupuncture treatments for pain ailments they can't fix through chiropractic medicine.

CASE STUDY It began in 1994 in a garage in Bellevue, Washington. Some high-tech gadget company, you ask? No. It was Amazon.com.

In the mid-to-late 1990s when we were running workshops on business renewal, we could surprise people with the answer to the question, "What is the largest bookstore in the country?" When we told them it was a "web company," they were fascinated (and skeptical). After all, don't you need to touch the books before you buy them?

Now when we ask the question, "What does Amazon sell?" people answer "books." Then they start to question the simplicity of their answer. They know it's more, but few know how much more.

Amazon has been on a quest to capture as much of your wallet as possible, and they seem to be doing a pretty good job. Consider this timeline:

- **1994**—They sell books.
- **1997**—They sell CDs and movies and hit almost $16 million in revenue.
- **1998**—They sell software, electronics, video games, toys, and home improvement items.
- **1999**—They hit $1 billion in revenue.
- **2001**—They ally with TravelStore.com.
- **2002**—They earn their first quarterly profit.
- **2003**—They ally with the NBA, Target, Toys-R-Us, and Old Navy.
- **2005**—They buy BookSurge for people who want to publish their own books.
- **2006**—They ally with DrugStore.com and begin selling groceries.
- **2007**—They launch the Kindle, an electronic book download and reading device.

Here's the bottom line. If it can be sold online, you can expect Amazon to sell it. When you think "share of wallet," who does it better than Amazon?

What is interesting about Amazon is how proactive they are at going after share of wallet. They could have ridden books all the way through maturity. Instead they expanded into other lines well before they were forced to do so.

CLUES

Does another business take your product or service and bundle it with their own offering? Do your clients ask for your help in finding other professionals? Do you talk with customers, listen to their issues, and say to yourself, "I could handle that"? Does someone else service your equipment, even though you could easily do so?

CHALLENGES

Building Share of Wallet requires that you provide goods or services that you are not presently producing. These may, in turn, require you to develop or acquire a new set of competencies. You must identify these new skills and then develop or acquire the assets needed to bring them to reality.

ASSUMPTIONS

You are assuming you can provide goods and services better or cheaper and still make a profit. You are also assuming your customers want a single supplier and that they will not squeeze you for a volume discount if they buy the full range of your offerings.

RISKS

There are two major risks associated with this strategy. First, your operating costs might exceed the revenues from your new offerings. Second, your customers might prefer to shop from several vendors rather than just one and may reject your offer of expanded products or services.

Renewal Strategy 8: Shift to the Sweet Spot

Why did IBM shift its strategy from making computer hardware to providing services? Because they could make more money by doing so. They would certainly like it if customers bought only IBM computers, but given the range of competition in the field, that is not realistic. So they focused on the part of the business where they could generate the highest profit margins—services and systems integration.

Think about your business and the total available market. Could you shift assets and talent to a more profitable place?

CASE STUDY Trader Joe's started as Pronto Markets and competed in the convenience store industry with 7-Eleven. They carried products similar to what other convenience stores carried. But without 7-Eleven's financial strength, their ability to expand was limited.

So they changed the game and their name and moved to the Sweet Spot. They decided not to go head to head against either convenience stores or standard supermarkets. Instead they created something new and highly profitable—a shopping adventure centered on their private label products.

Trader Joe's creates this adventure through fun and cheekiness. Their uniforms are colorful Hawaiian shirts. And it has created linked but cute private-label names for its foods focused on ethnicity: Trader José's, Trader Ming's, Arabian Joe's, and Trader Joe-San, for example.

Rather than carry the full line of food products that can be found in many stores (and that carry very low margins), the company's leaders chose to develop and carry specialty, private-labeled products, which can only be purchased at Trader Joe's. The stores continuously rotate ten to fifteen new items in each week and make room for them by eliminating the same number of older items. Thus, rather than being a predictable grocery store, which always has the standard offerings, Trader Joe's has become a shopping adventure and has created the "Treasure Hunt." Customers seek treasures that can only be found at Trader Joe's and that last for only a limited time.

Trade Joe's does not try to be the best at everything. In fact, the company's approach leaves it at a disadvantage in four key areas:

- You can't go into Trader Joe's and purchase a complete market basket of groceries.
- The company's prices tend to be higher than many other stores.
- Trader Joe's carries very few national brands.
- The stores tend to be in weak locations in aging or rundown shopping centers.

But the treasure hunt and adventure aspects outweigh these weaknesses. Whether a customer is looking for wine, organic herbs, organic rice, dried fruits, imported cheeses, hummus, or frozen chocolate croissants, Trader Joe's will always have something that interests them. And they sell high-margin products unavailable elsewhere.

This focus on the sweet spot has delivered financially for Trader Joe's. Their revenue per square foot is more than twice the industry average. By resisting the call to sell everything and focusing on the sweet spot, Trader Joe's has created a winning model in the grocery industry.

CLUES

The biggest clue is that your offerings are becoming commoditized. This happens when you can't differentiate them or when the competition adds so much capacity that even differentiated offerings can't gain a price premium. A second hint that you should consider this strategy is that competitors are making money in niches you could fill.

CHALLENGES

Like some of the earlier strategies, the challenge here is one of timing. Move too soon and you may find a sweet spot that is too small to support you. Move too late and you may be just "part of the crowd."

ASSUMPTIONS

By adopting this strategy you are assuming that there is an uncontested or lightly contested market that exists and can be profitable. In their book *Blue Ocean Strategy*, authors W. Chan Kim and Renée Mauborgne use Cirque de Soleil (Cirque) as an example of moving to an uncontested space. Cirque was created in 1984 by an accordion-playing stilt walker and a group of street performers who wanted to reinvent the circus. Their goal was to simultaneously lower costs and increase differentiation in the declining circus industry. Twenty-five years later they have proven the wisdom of their choice.

RISKS

Cirque du Soleil took a risk that its form of entertainment, different from anything that had come before it, would find a large enough audience. Traditional circuses focused on kids, whereas Cirque sought to entertain the whole family. Circuses have animal acts, Cirque saw animal acts as too expensive. Circuses had star performers, Cirque did not want to rely on stars. Cirque succeeded, but there are significant risks associated with this strategy. You may be breaking new ground, with no corporate experience to draw on. If you've miscalculated the existence of the sweet spot, you may think you are moving to a blue ocean only to find it a barren desert.

Renewal Strategy 9: Leverage Your Core Competencies

To what other use can you apply your skills and assets? That's the question that triggers consideration of this strategy. Consider Honda. They excel in the design and manufacture of internal combustion engines. But they reorganized their company to find other uses for those engines besides cars: motorcycles, lawnmowers, snow blowers, generator sets, jet skis, and more. Consider Marriott Corporation. They excel in "hospitality." Some time ago, they put their skills to work managing retirement centers.

CASE STUDY They started as Timely Publications in 1939. In the 1950s they became Atlas Comics. And in 1961, the first *Fantastic Four* comic put Marvel Comics on the map of cultural icons for a whole generation of young (mostly) men. Since then, they have been known as Marvel Comics, Marvel Studios, and Marvel Entertainment Group.

Marvel was purchased in 1989 for $82.5 million and filed for Chapter 11 bankruptcy in 1996. Twenty years later, in 2009, Disney offered to purchase them for $4 billion. On the surface we can see that combining Disney's distribution capabilities with Marvel's licensing know-how makes sense. But is it worth $4 billion?

Marvel has been able to renew itself because of a core competency that can't be duplicated—they own over 5,000 "characters," and these characters have ongoing value.

Think about Marvel in the context of the definition of a core competency:

- It provides **consumer benefits**. Do we see benefits in "entertainment"? We sure do, and we are willing to spend a lot of money "being entertained."
- It is **not easy to imitate**. Once a "comic hero" captures our imagination everything else is a cheap knockoff.
- It can be **leveraged widely** into many products and markets. Take a look at what Marvel has done with its characters. The company has put them on television, in films, at a theme park in Dubai, in video games, and even in role-playing games.

Look at all of the competencies you possess. Can you find a Captain America in your stable of competencies? If so, how else can you leverage him?

CLUES

Look at the world through the lens of your core competencies. Sometimes your own people will say, "We could do that." That's an important indication that you can put their skills to work in a way you've not done before. Sometimes you will see a problem in another industry and say to yourself, "Well, if I were running that company I'd . . ." Sometimes the spark comes from a supplier who sees your capabilities in ways you don't.

CHALLENGES

The biggest challenge is while some businesses may appear to require the same skill set, the actual skills required for success may be very different in practice. Running a hotel and a retirement center have a lot of similar attributes, but each presents unique problems.

ASSUMPTIONS

This strategy assumes that competencies can be transplanted into a different business setting. It further assumes your competencies will be strong enough to overwhelm entrenched and more experienced competition.

RISKS

You might underestimate the cost of dealing with different business settings and find yourself in an unprofitable situation. You might also overestimate the power of your competencies and find others can do it better in a particular industry than you can.

Transformation Group
(New Customers / New Assets)

Renewal Strategy 10: Declare Victory and Move On

What do Berkshire Hathaway, Illinois Tool Works, and Dean Kamen have in common? They all use the essence of Declare Victory and Move On. They continue to operate and grow by taking proceeds from the operations or money from the sale of existing assets to fund new growth. Berkshire Hathaway (run by the legendary Warren Buffet) doesn't simply hold underperforming stocks in the hope that eventually they'll improve. It sells them to buy (hopefully) better-performing stocks.

Illinois Tool Works is a global company of over 800 business units that are left to run in a mostly autonomous fashion. If a business unit does not meet performance objectives, the company sells it and makes new acquisitions.

Dean Kamen is a serial inventor who uses proceeds from earlier inventions to start dramatically new businesses. Employing proceeds from medical inventions such as stents and portable insulin pumps, Kamen invented and developed the Segway personal transportation device.

CASE STUDY Industries evolve and eventually reach the end of their useful lives. That is what happened to the Reading Railway (yes, the same Reading Railway that is in Monopoly).

The Reading Railway was founded in 1833 as a horse-drawn railway for hauling coal. It grew over time and by 1871 was the single largest company in the world. But over time, the attractiveness of transporting coal by rail diminished, and Reading's value decreased. In 1976 the bulk of the railway was merged into Conrail. Reading was left with 650 real estate assets along with some coal and out-of-use right-of-ways.

Reading was then acquired by the Craig Companies, which owned a chain of movie theaters in Australia and New Zealand. After selling off the rail assets Craig Companies changed its name and became Reading International. They now own and operate cinema chains and live theaters in the United States, Australia, New Zealand, and Puerto Rico.

Unlike other cinema chains, Reading International focuses much of its capital on real estate. It invests its cash flow from its cinema business and uses it to buy properties for additional locations. Since the company owns the land rather than leasing it, Reading is never in danger of being evicted to make way for a new tenant.

The owners of Reading International profit from ticket sales at their box offices as well as investing in long-term real estate appreciation. Though the company left the railroad business it stayed true to its real estate roots.

The Reading Railroad lasted for 150 years, but all businesses eventually reach their end. Rather than riding to its inevitable decline, the new owners of Reading International declared victory and used the value remaining in the railroad company to build a growing business with more relevance for today and tomorrow.

CLUES

Entrepreneurs often feel the need to move on when the thrill of building a business is replaced with the tough slog of running it. Experienced business people often look for opportunities to prove themselves in a new setting. In either case, if you feel there is something better to do with your time, your talent, or your assets, perhaps there is.

CHALLENGES

Businesses and individuals face the same challenges—having enough cash on-hand to invest and having the time to find the next business to develop. You also may face the choice of leaving a high-paying and stable field for one with much less stability and greater risk of outright failure. There is also the ongoing challenge of having to learn about new technologies, industries, or markets.

ASSUMPTIONS

This strategy is based on the assumption that the urge to move on is based on real opportunities and not just dissatisfaction with the status quo. You are also assuming that you have the skill set to win in a different field. This strategy may be exciting to consider, but it takes more than amateur interest to succeed.

RISKS

The risk here is that you may give up on something with reasonable revenue and return for hoped-for, but unknown, returns. Dean Kamen's Segway has not lived up to its original goal of "revolutionizing transportation." On the other hand, Illinois Tool Works only buys operating companies they think can perform better under their management and direction. Do you have the cash to sustain you while you move on? Have you realistically estimated the amount of time it will take to find and develop the next opportunity?

Renewal Strategy 11: Keep the Knowledge; Switch the Business

Look at newsreels from the 1950s and you would come to the conclusion that by the end of the twentieth century all of our electric power would be produced by nuclear power plants. However, the reactor accidents at Three Mile Island in 1970 and at Chernobyl in 1986 put a freeze on the construction of nuclear power plants. Governments around the world cancelled contracts for new nukes and switched to tried-and-true (and safe) fossil fuel plants.

Did Westinghouse and General Electric, the leaders in nuclear power plant construction go out of business? No. Given their knowledge of the industry they shifted their business to maintenance and refueling of existing nuclear plants and are well placed to resume construction activities when the time is right.

Go to a much smaller scale and consider the building inspectors for your city or village. Many of them are former plumbers, electricians, and carpenters who no longer work in the trades but use their knowledge for a new role. Tom Peters, the head of The Tom Peters Company, took his knowledge of strategy gained from consulting to large corporations and turned it into a very profitable writing and speaking career. His company has now come full circle and is back in the consulting business.

CASE STUDY 3M is a science-based company that lets knowledge lead it to new businesses. As such, we regard it as the quintessential user of this strategy.

3M was founded in 1902 by five businessmen mining a mineral deposit for grinding-wheel abrasives. The deposits proved to be of little value, so instead they focused on sandpaper products. Early technical and marketing innovations produced successes, and 3M kept changing to take advantage of what they learned. When you look at the company's history, you see that it continues to renew itself by building on knowledge it already has.

- In the 1920s, 3M developed the world's first waterproof sandpaper for automotive use.
- In 1925, a young lab assistant invented masking tape, starting a series of adhesive products.
- The 1940s saw the creation of Scotchlite™ Reflective Sheeting, magnetic sound recording tape, filament adhesive tape, and offset printing plates.

- The 1950s brought Thermo-Fax™ copying process, Scotchgard™ Fabric Protector, videotape, Scotch-Brite® Cleaning Pads, and new electro-mechanical products.
- The 1960s saw them move into medical and dental products.
- Pharmaceuticals, radiology, and energy control came in the 1970s
- They introduced Post-it® Notes, in 1980, which created a whole new category in the marketplace and changed people's communication and organization habits.
- In the 1990s, new products included immune-response modifier pharmaceuticals; brightness-enhancement films for electronic displays; and flexible circuits used in inkjet printers, cell phones, and other electronic devices.

3M now has six distinct business units ranging from office supplies to health care to protection services. Their chairman refers to them as being "science-based." As such, they continually build on existing knowledge to develop new products and new businesses.

CLUES

Look at knowledge that is unique to you or your company or your industry.

- Could you use this knowledge to forward-integrate and create something larger? (Magna International went from automotive components to sub-assemblies, to assemblies, to total vehicle assembly.)
- Could you use this knowledge and backward-integrate? (Panasonic moving from a user of batteries to a supplier of batteries for advanced devices.)

- Could you use this knowledge in another industry? Experienced executives switch companies and industries all the time, bringing their knowledge and skills with them.

CHALLENGES

Will new customers believe you? In the 1960s IBM was a "manufacturing" company that created closed systems (i.e., all IBM components and sub-systems). IBM saw the opportunity to build on their knowledge of how computers and information technology were used. They created IBM Consulting in the late 1980s with the intention of moving from manufacturing to business services. However, it took a while before customers accepted that the company representatives would give objective (and non-IBM focused) recommendations. Over time IBM proved that they could do so, but cash was flowing in the wrong direction for their first few years of this new business.

ASSUMPTIONS

The assumption here is that you have the deep knowledge that allows you to move to other settings. There is a second assumption that your knowledge is applicable outside the boundaries of your current business model.

RISKS

The primary risk is that you switch into a business in which either your knowledge proves inadequate or that has significant other barriers that stand in the way of your success. Additionally, you may have to develop new competencies and will consume a lot of time and money doing so.

Renewal Strategy 12: Cash Out and Double Down

Could one of your product lines or business units really excel if it was given the resources and management attention it needs for spectacular growth? Are you diffusing your talent when you might get better results by focusing it? You may want to consider selling marginal units or shifting money away from them and investing the proceeds in businesses that show greater promise.

CASE STUDY In 1972, the pharmaceutical giant Eli Lilly purchased Pacemakers Inc. for $127 million and renamed it Guidant. Guidant competes with Medtronic and St. Jude Medical in the medical device industry.

By the 1990s, medical devices were responsible for about 20 percent of Eli Lilly's revenues. But Eli Lilly was having problems. It was trailing other firms on international presence, and many of its key patents had expired. Its core pharmaceutical business was in trouble. It needed to invest more in its core, but it didn't have the money to do so.

In order to generate the investment needed for its core, the leadership of Eli Lilly sold off Guidant. Guidant competes in health care, just as Eli Lilly does. But the two businesses are very different.

Medical devices (such as pacemakers, defibrillators, and stents) have relatively short lifecycles and require timely decision making. On the other hand, developing and winning approval for pharmaceutical drugs mandates a much longer timeline. It is quite challenging for a single company to be able to operate at these two different speeds.

In 2006, Eli Lilly cashed out of Guidant so it could double down on its core pharmaceutical business. After entertaining multiple bids from Johnson and Johnson and Boston Scientific, Eli Lilly sold Guidant to Boston Scientific for $27 billion. This sale did two things: It raised a tremendous amount of cash to invest in drug development. And it freed up management time and attention to focus on the core business.

Should the executives of Eli Lilly look upon Guidant as a failure because they sold it? Because they could not make it work? Hardly. They received a magnificent price for an asset that was not essential to their overall business success. They used the proceeds from this divestiture to strengthen their core pharmaceutical business.

CLUES

You might see that one of your business units is growth-constrained because it lacks resources. You might realize that you are spending precious resources on one product line while denying resources to another, newly-introduced line. You might realize that one of your businesses is in a profitless industry.

For example, general hospitals tend to have very low profits. They must invest broadly in order to offer a wide range of services, and so end up with underused assets. To combat this, companies have been creating specialty hospitals, such as the Cleveland Clinic, a "heart hospital," and Johns Hopkins, a "cancer hospital."

CHALLENGES

The challenge here is to agree to let go of something you may have grown from a start-up. Business leaders take intense pride in what they have accomplished and are reluctant to drop it.

ASSUMPTIONS

You are assuming that you have long-term opportunities in one of your remaining business units. You are further assuming that the key to its success is an infusion of cash and other company resources. Finally, you are assuming that although the business you are trying to sell contributes limited value to your portfolio you will still find a buyer willing to pay for it.

RISKS

This strategy depends on your ability to make two good decisions. First, you must be sure you are cashing out of a business that does not belong in your portfolio. If the business could succeed with better management, provide those resources and leave it alone.

Second, you must choose the right business in which to invest the proceeds from your cashing out. Look to the future and make sure you are not basing this decision solely on historical performance. Sony's stellar run with the Walkman line of products may have prevented them from shifting R&D funds from electro-mechanical products to software and solid-state products in time to deal with music downloads and the dominance of Apple.

Time to Choose

Renewing your business starts with plenty of reflection. However, you can't think forever. It's now time to choose your path to renew your business. That is the topic of the next chapter.

CHAPTER SEVEN

Choosing the Best Renewal Alternative

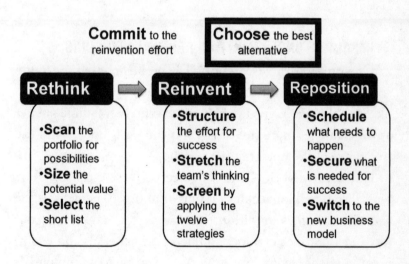

Commit to the reinvention effort   **Choose** the best alternative

Rethink ⟹ **Reinvent** ⟹ **Reposition**

- **Scan** the portfolio for possibilities
- **Size** the potential value
- **Select** the short list

- **Structure** the effort for success
- **Stretch** the team's thinking
- **Screen** by applying the twelve strategies

- **Schedule** what needs to happen
- **Secure** what is needed for success
- **Switch** to the new business model

There are two steps to choosing the best renewal alternatives. First, evaluate how each of your alternatives rates on each of the value measures you care about. Second, obtain leadership commitment to the chosen direction.

Evaluating Your Renewal Alternatives

For the most part, organizations need little help with the quantitative evaluation of their opportunities. Whether through the use of spreadsheets or financial evaluation packages, management knows how to calculate financial metrics such as short- and long-term cash flows, Net Present Value (NPV), Return on Investment (ROI), and Economic Value Added (EVA).

But there are two topics that are critical to the evaluation of renewal alternatives that are typically less well understood. They are the impact of uncertainty and the evaluation of non-financial value measures.

IMPACT OF UNCERTAINTY ON RENEWAL DECISIONS

Organizations crave certainty. The problem is that the future consists of uncertainties. Study it as much and as long as you like; you'll never come up with an absolutely infallible answer as to what the future holds. All you can do is understand the true range of the uncertainties you face.

Consider what goes into engineering cost estimates. The typical standard for accuracy is plus or minus 10 percent. If the actual cost comes in within that range, you have done your job. Organizations can lock in quotes on materials and equipment to further reduce uncertainty. So getting to within plus or minus 10 percent is within the realm of possibility for routine cost estimates.

But the same is not true for estimating marketing uncertainties. Suppose you introduce a new service. It could be a dud and sell almost nothing, or it could skyrocket. The underlying uncertainty is no longer plus or minus 10 percent. Instead, it might be plus 300 percent on the upside and minus 85 percent on the downside. If that is the real range, how could you give a plus or minus 10 percent estimate on projected sales and keep a straight face?

Companies often underestimate the risks that go along with their renewal initiatives. Because they underestimate the uncertainty they face, they also undervalue flexibility and contingency planning.

Incorporating the impact of uncertainty is particularly important for renewal decisions because such choices have wider ranges of risk than do operational uncertainties. You have years of accumulated data and relevant experience to reduce your uncertainty on operating estimates. But you probably have little or no relevant data about your renewal alternative.

If you think about uncertainties (both on the upside and on the downside) as ranges rather than specific answers, you'll change the questions you ask. The answers arising from these questions lead to new insights. For example, consider the following:

- Given the renewal uncertainties you face, should you add capacity before it is needed so you can handle fast growth, or should you hold off and add it only after demand has been demonstrated?
- What can you invest in today at modest cost that would enable you to triple your investment six months faster than you otherwise could if the renewed business really takes off?
- How long will it be before your renewed line of business is made obsolete by competitors launching products with more attractive value propositions?

Evaluation of Nonfinancial Value Measures

Financial data are always important. But they are not the only things that matter. To properly choose one alternative over another you must look at the full range of financial and non-financial, quantifiable and non-quantifiable objectives. As Albert Einstein is reported to have said: "Not everything that can be counted counts, and not everything that counts can be counted."

To make high-quality renewal decisions we need to understand the objectives that really matter. To do this we ask, "Who are the players, and what do they want?" A player is an individual or (more often) a group who will be affected by a renewal decision. There are usually multiple players, and each player will have a different set of decision criteria and may place different weightings on the relative importance of their criteria.

In Chapter 4, we discussed the seven attributes of high-quality decisions. To achieve quality in Objectives you must first determine who the players are who have a stake in renewal and then determine what they hope to achieve. Let's examine this in a bit more detail.

A list of potential players could include: customers, shareholders, partners, CEO/founder/Executive Committee, division management, functional management, workforce, unions, suppliers, national and local governments, regulators, and environmental groups. The challenge is to narrow this list to the four or five whose perspectives are most relevant to the renewal decision. These players become the columns in your player table.

The rows in the table are the wants of each player, starting with the most important on the top row. Typically you will define four or five wants for each player.

Here is an example of the players' chart for a family-owned company with professional management:

Who Are the Players?

	Non-Employee Family Owners	Executive Team	Future Leaders / Next Generation	Workforce
Most Important	Steady cash flow	Ability to build competitive advantage	Balance between authority and responsibility	Job security
	Be there for the next generation of family members	Ability to attract and retain top talent	Work / life balance	Competitive pay
	Don't tarnish the family name	Short-term and long-term wealth accumulation	Rewards based on delivered results as opposed to seniority	Reasonable hours and safe working conditions
Lesser Importance			Opportunity for career advancement	Attractive benefits package

(Left axis label: What Do They Want?)

Who Are the Players, and What Do They Want?

Note that not all wants are consistent, either between players or even within a single player. The Non-Employee Family Owners want steady cash flow for themselves, and they also want the company to be there for their sons and daughters. To achieve the second, they may need to take risks that imperil the first.

Once you have identified the players' objectives you can do two things. First, you can use the criteria to revise your choices so that they deliver more of what people want. For example, the Future Leaders/Next Generation want rewards based on merit and a balance between authority and responsibility. If you push responsibility and accountability further down in the organization, this will help deliver on these desires.

It is a hard truth that not everyone will get all of what they want, and in some cases, they will not get any of what they want. For example, the workforce wants job security and competitive pay. By *competitive pay*, they mean wages that compare favorably with those of other U.S. workers in the industry. But if the organization is now in direct competition with Chinese or Indian labor, *competitive pay* may not mean what workers think it means.

Use your decision criteria to evaluate your renewal alternatives. This will involve both quantitative and qualitative assessments. Some criteria (such as cash flow and competitive pay and benefits) lend themselves to credible quantification. Other criteria will be more difficult to quantify and are best ranked qualitatively. In our example above these include the ability to build competitive advantage, the ability to attract and retain top talent, the balance between authority and responsibility, and work/life balance.

Choosing and Committing to the Preferred Renewal Alternative

By this point you have developed and evaluated a set of renewal alternatives. Now you must align your leadership team behind the new direction and actually make the renewal decision. Like the Commit decision made between Rethink and Reinvent, you must make the renewal decision a high-quality choice. Remember our red-yellow-green method? Before you choose your renewal path, each of the seven attributes that are part of this decision need to be green. If necessary, review the approach presented in detail in Chapter 4.

As a final test before committing to a renewal alternative we suggest you think about the following list of common decision traps:

- *Anchoring*—Did you "fall in love" with your first idea for renewing the company? Have you let this blind you to other ideas?
- *Settling*—Did you consider the full range of alternatives from mild to wild, or did you just stop at mild plus?
- *Confirming evidence*—Did you see only what you wanted to see? Have you collected "evidence" that supports only your favorite idea for renewal?
- *Groupthink*—Did you listen to dissenting points of view, or did you staff the effort entirely with those who already think the same way as you?
- *Unintended consequences*—All decisions create new problems. Have you tried to envision the kinds of problems renewal might create?
- *Sunk cost*—Are you moving forward simply to protect all the time and money you have already invested?

If you have fallen into one or more of these traps, go back and rectify the situation before committing to a renewal alternative.

The decision about how to renew your business is a rational one, but it must take into account emotional and cultural perspectives as well. If you neglect the rational perspective, you will have trouble selling your solution to your board and the market. If you neglect the emotional perspective, you will obtain surface agreement but not the deep commitment you need for successful execution. And if you neglect the cultural perspective, you will have a difficult time getting everyone to pull in the selected direction.

Here are some of the questions that must be answered concerning each of these three perspectives:

RATIONAL

- What is the risk and return of your preferred alternative?
- What does the cash flow profile look like?
- How would your cash flow change in an optimistic scenario? In a pessimistic scenario?
- What specific investments will you make to execute the strategy?
- What changes do you need in your workforce (e.g., capability upgrades and/or switching personnel)?
- Do you need to change your organizational structure or redefine your profit centers to successfully execute your choice?

EMOTIONAL

- How can you deal with the initial surprise and uncertainty some customers/partners/suppliers/distributors may feel when they hear of your plans?
- How can you bring the people on board who see themselves as losing ground with the selected alternative?
- How will you deal with those workers who feel hurt or betrayed by the new direction?
- What could you do to build emotional ties to your new direction?

- How can you motivate those who will remain with the legacy organization and who know that the end of their operations is in sight no matter how hard they work?
- How can you reassure your clients/customers that the new direction will benefit them?

CULTURAL

- How can you celebrate your past while moving into the future?
- What parts of your choice threaten your existing culture?
- How can you explain to those who came before you why the change makes sense?
- What should you modify in your selected plan to make it more culturally acceptable to your organization?
- What changes do you need to make in your culture moving forward?

Once the renewal choice has been made, the work of leading both the new business and the legacy business begins. How to do so effectively is the topic of the next chapter on Repositioning.

PART III

RE**THINK**
RE**INVENT**
RE**POSITION**

CHAPTER EIGHT

Making the Transition to the New Business Model

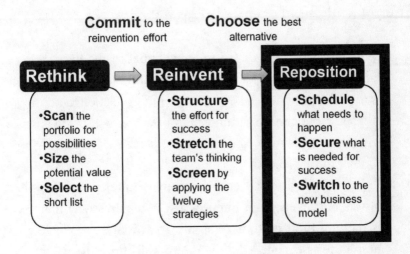

Commit to the reinvention effort

Choose the best alternative

Rethink
- **Scan** the portfolio for possibilities
- **Size** the potential value
- **Select** the short list

Reinvent
- **Structure** the effort for success
- **Stretch** the team's thinking
- **Screen** by applying the twelve strategies

Reposition
- **Schedule** what needs to happen
- **Secure** what is needed for success
- **Switch** to the new business model

Executing Your Renewal Strategy

In *Rethink* you examined the Renewal possibilities in your portfolio and decided which of your business units merited a renewal initiative. In *Reinvent* you created a short list of attractive alternative strategies and selected the right one for your organization. Now you have to make it happen. You have to *Reposition* your business.

Three Components of Repositioning

Like the other two phases of the renewal process, Repositioning has three distinct but interrelated parts.

1. **Schedule** the changes: Consider what has to change to bring about renewal and identify the portfolio of projects necessary to bring about these changes. Strategy is not something that just happens. You must plan how you will bring about the needed changes, and the way to do this is by identifying one or more projects.
2. **Secure** your assets: Renewal often requires new tangible assets but, even more importantly, it requires new human, structural, and customer capital. In this step you'll determine the assets needed for your renewal effort and will allocate them accordingly.
3. **Switch** to the new business model: This is the hard work of keeping the old business model alive and viable while you transition to new customers or provide a new set of offerings to initialize the new business model.

Schedule

Serious renewal requires that you undertake a portfolio of projects in order to start the changes moving. Since a desired change always triggers other, less desirable, changes, now is a good time to think about unintended consequences that could flow from your renewal strategy.

For example:

1. Perhaps your renewal strategy is based on moving your business to a new location to better serve your clientele. How will this affect your workforce? Will they move? Will it cause problems for your suppliers? How will competitors react?
2. Perhaps your renewal strategy is based on converting from an eight-hour workday to a twenty-four-hour operation. How will this affect your procedures for equipment maintenance? How will workers get to and from work at "night owl" hours? Will community relationships have to be addressed because of noise or traffic?
3. Perhaps your renewal strategy is based on selling off most of your existing business and focusing on your smallest, but highest-growth business. What contracts will you have to amend or break? How will you deal with systems designed for a multiunit business now that you no longer have one?

The work of Reposition is broken down into manageable projects. Following are potential projects to consider for each of the twelve strategies. Please note that these are only general suggestions. When you reposition your business, you will have to develop the custom portfolio of projects that best fit your particular needs.

New Concept Group
(Existing Customers / Existing Assets)

STRATEGY 1: CATCH THE NEW WAVE

Shifting your current business to the next hot thing often takes you beyond your current understanding of what your customers want and need. The key here is to modify your business to stay aligned with your customers as their needs evolve. What if your local diner had caught the premium coffee wave in time? Might they have kept customers from deserting them?

Here are a few projects that you might find useful as you Catch the New Wave.

Do market research—You need to uncover emerging needs before they are well satisfied by your competitors. Whether you do this formally or informally, you need to keep an eye on the marketplace and anticipate future needs and wants. Do you know what your leading edge customers are saying? Southwest Airlines is using Twitter to drive the conversation with its customers so they can better understand their evolving needs.

Gain competitive intelligence—You will need to study your existing and emerging competitors. Ask your sales force, "Whose turf are we entering? How do we expect existing competitors to respond if we press up against them?" Also ask, "Who is new in our competitive landscape?" Remember, Sears Roebuck and Company (a "department store") did not initially consider Wal-Mart (a "discounter") as a serious competitor. Today Sears has ceded huge swaths of its customer base to Wal-Mart and has little hope of recapturing them.

Remodel/retool—More often than not Catching the New Wave will require that you change and upgrade your "packaging." You see this in the redecorating that accompanies a significant menu change at a renewed restaurant. You see this in the green packaging used for the new organic food products. You must send signals to your customers that something has changed.

STRATEGY 2: PUT OLD WINE IN NEW BOTTLES

Sometimes you have good products and services and (potentially) loyal customers but you seem a bit dated. Now might be the right time to repackage or rebrand your offerings to revive them.

Here are a few projects that you might want to consider as you Put Old Wine in New Bottles.

Rebrand the product—To stay current with customers' wants and needs you may end up buying or creating a new product or service and incorporating it into your identity. Visio was a graphic competitor to Microsoft's suite of offerings until Microsoft bought the company and rebranded it as Microsoft Visio. Microsoft had been losing business to Visio, but Visio did not have the marketing clout to grow as quickly as its technical merits would justify. Rebranding the technically superior product as part of the Microsoft Office suite gave it the presence and funding necessary to accelerate its growth.

Update your marketing message—In the middle of 2008, the United States was in gas-price sticker shock. Ford and GM rapidly shifted their messages from "bigger and more powerful" to "greener and more efficient." Their customer base had changed and, although they maintained essentially the same stable of cars and trucks as previously, they tried to stay relevant by changing the emphasis of their message. Admittedly this is only a stopgap strategy to employ when the market changes quickly and you need time to create new offerings. As we saw in 2009, GM ran out of time and filed for bankruptcy. Ford, on the other hand, seems to be adjusting (barely) in time.

Renew your facility—Sometimes you simply need to modernize the look and features of your place of business. A local café might install free Wi-Fi to avoid losing good customers to the new coffee shop down the block.

STRATEGY 3: REVISE YOUR PROFIT MODEL

There are stories of companies or even entire industries that fell on hard times because customer needs changed and the firms did not react quickly enough. Financial planners were under pressure for "churning" their customers' accounts and making unnecessary trades to earn commissions. By switching their profit model to charging a flat percentage of assets under management they removed this conflict of interest and better aligned themselves with their customers' interests.

As you Revise Your Profit Model, you might find the following projects in your portfolio.

Review the future of the industry—Managers are pretty good at dealing with in-your-face problems and opportunities. On the other hand, they are often bad at foreseeing slow, incremental changes. Because most of your organizations have spent the past fifteen or so years becoming "lean and mean," your staff is probably overworked. This leaves them little opportunity to ponder the future of your business environment. We suggest you take some time to investigate the edge of your mental radar screen and consider the opportunities and problems that will confront your business as you move into the future.

In the early 1990s, Microsoft was running full out to dominate desktop computer applications when a group of middle managers noted the arrival of something called the *Internet*. In a stunningly short time for a company its size, Microsoft shifted to address the implications of the Net and quickly overtook Netscape with its Internet Explorer browser.

Conduct an in-depth strategy review—Strategy deals with how you will accomplish the goals you have set or accepted for your business in order to make a profit. First of all, can you and your workers articulate the goals that define the potential for both short- and long-term profitability for your business? Second, will your present business model help you achieve both sets of goals? Third, what could you do to make changes in how you get paid for your goods and services?

Enable technological changes—As you embark on changes to your profit model you should revisit the technologies you use to conduct business. Newspapers are a current example of a business profit model that *has* to react to new technologies. Likewise, we're pretty sure that most of our readers can be reached 24/7 without having a landline-based telephone. This is too bad for many of the traditional phone companies, but they had their chance to aggressively move into mobile and most didn't do so.

Extension Group (New Customers / Existing Assets)

STRATEGY 4: AIM HIGHER OR LOWER

As you try to move significantly up-market or down-market to serve new customers, you will have to overcome your own notions about "who buys our stuff." In order to Aim Higher or Lower you might involve your teams in one or more of the following projects.

Find luxury/economy crossover customers—As you consider the upscale/downscale issue of extension, think about the strength of your brand and the potential impact of changing your audience. Can your brands move to new places? During the recession of 2009, BMW was able to partially counter the loss of business in its high-end flagship brand with interest in the trendy, cool (and down-market) Mini.

Make a cost analysis—Moving beyond your current customers is not cheap, especially if you cannot service these new customers from your existing facilities or with your existing sales force. Going up-market with Lexus was costly for Toyota. Profits lagged as the company incurred the expenses of building new manufacturing facilities and recruited a new sales force. Toyota needed the wherewithal to sustain several years of negative cash flow, but it paid off handsomely.

Rethink your marketing technology—Are you keeping customers in the dark about all of the new things you are bringing to them? If so, how will you rethink your marketing message? Many large corporations are now using Twitter, Facebook, and other social media as a way to communicate with potential customers.

STRATEGY 5: MAKE A TIME SHIFT

Can you do business during a new or different part of the day to reach different customers? McDonald's did, and now they pretty much own the breakfast time slot in the quick service restaurant business. If you have fixed assets that are only used during part of the day, you have underused assets. As you Make a Time Shift you will want to launch some of the following projects.

Research your customers' habits—What are your normal hours of operation? What other parts of the day might customers want your services? Can you open for business during "nontraditional" times and gain a profitable revenue stream? Make sure there is enough business to warrant the expenses associated with changed and /or extra hours.

Review your operations strategy—What will it take to provide profitable service during other time slots, and what current activities will have to be moved to a different time? Examine your total operation and look for the unintended consequences of doing business during a different part of the day. Will you have to shift maintenance tasks? When will you need to train new workers? Will previous off-hour operations get in the way of your new working hours?

Do a workforce analysis—Here's the key to making the time-shift strategy work: You already have the physical assets in place, but will you be able to get people to work during these new hours? How will the new schedule affect married workers? Retired workers? Students? Worker safety? Transportation issues? Remember, it may make sense to you, but you will probably not be the person working these new hours.

STRATEGY 6: GET A PERSONALITY TRANSPLANT

If you want to focus on new and emerging end-user needs, you may need to change the perception of your business. Harley Davidson did a nice job of keeping elements of the outlaw biker image alive (for example, the sound of a revving Harley motor is trademarked), but they also added a dash of respectability. In 1983, they started the Harley Owners Group (H.O.G.) club as a way for bikers to come together and ride as a "gang" for good causes. Good product—great personality transplant. As you Get a Personality Transplant for your own business we suggest that you consider the following projects.

Do a generations-based strategy review—Existing businesses often have an unconscious alignment with an entire generation. The renewal challenge for many businesses is coming to grips with the wants and needs of a different generation.

Cadillac did this brilliantly with the Cadillac CTS. The age profile of the Caddy driver in late 2009 is significantly younger than it was in 1989. The CTS is built on a platform too small for the traditional Caddy buyer, but perfect for the younger BMW driver the company wanted to win over. Cadillac knew it needed to appeal to a younger set of drivers and it changed the car to fit their wants and needs. Study who buys your product or service; understand who you *need* in the future.

Conduct a strategy review—The idea of a personality transplant may require you to go back to your business goals and the fundamental strategy you use to achieve these goals. You have been advised for years that "you can't be all things to all people." However, when it comes to this renewal option you have to ask yourself if you can be meaningful to another group of customers.

Redefine your business—When someone asks you to describe your business, how do you start? Do you focus on what you do or who you serve? Whereas modifying your profit model may get you to consider how you go about running your business, considering a personality transplant will force you to reconsider your very identity as a business.

Solutions Group (Existing Customers / New Assets)

STRATEGY 7: BUILD SHARE OF WALLET

Your existing customers certainly have more wants and needs than you are currently satisfying. Therefore it may make sense to move toward becoming a one-stop shop. Think about it. Has your favorite dry cleaner become your tailor over the years? Have you found that the local brake shop is just fine for a tune up? It's good for you (saves you another trip) and it's good for them (increases their revenue). Manufacturing companies have been working this angle for years as they move more and more into the solutions business. Consider some of these projects as you Build Share of Wallet.

Perform a customer value-chain analysis—You can choose where on the value chain you want to compete and where you do not. Understanding your customers' value chain allows you to see what you can provide in addition to what you already supply to them. This also gives you the opportunity to consider the move to higher-margin products and services. Cell phone manufacturers get it. Not only do we get a telephone, but they also "give" us a camera, MP3 player, stopwatch, calendar, and other goodies. All in one package.

"Skate to where the puck will be"—Wayne Gretzky, the great hockey player from the 1990s, attributed his success to this maxim. He succeeded by sensing when and where to intercept the puck. Part of grabbing a larger share of your customers' wallets will come from understanding their future wants and needs, not just from assuming those will be the same as their current needs. This requires a solid understanding of your customers' industries and a commitment to spending the time and resources to consider how they might be changing.

STRATEGY 8: SHIFT TO THE SWEET SPOT

Value migration may explain the increase or decrease in your margins as your customers' priorities evolve and are met by other offerings. Years ago we saw the migration of margins from PC manufacturers to software companies. Accounting firms' value shifted from audits to consulting. Exiting commodity businesses and moving into specialty businesses is fine general advice, but the question is, "Which specialty businesses?" Consider the following projects as you Shift to the Sweet Spot.

Review your customer ranks—Not all customers are good customers. Doctors complain of patients who waste time talking about symptoms unrelated to their main complaints. Retailers have customers who return almost everything they buy. Sometimes the best thing you can do for your business is to "fire" certain customers or, at least, make it harder for them to do business with you. Given that you have limited time and resources, you must deploy them for the benefit of those customers for whom they will do the most good.

The challenge here is to segregate customers by profitability and eliminate those with a negative overall contribution.

Redefine geography—Sometimes you may find the sweet spot in a different part of the city and sometimes you have to move to another country. Your customers migrate; you might have to as well. Watch geographic and demographic shifts of your customer base, your supplier base, and your workforce.

Explore adjacent profit pools—Your customers spend their money across a series of "pools" that you should consider tapping. For example, people who buy a boat also spend money on financing the deal, buying insurance, maintaining the boat, and tricking it out with modifications. Boat dealers try to participate in all of these pools to gather more of their customers' money. However, they also use their capabilities to grab new customers for special services. Your local shipyard wants your maintenance business, whether you bought the boat from them or not.

STRATEGY 9: LEVERAGE YOUR CORE COMPETENCIES

The concept of *core competency* was brought to the attention of businesses through the work of Gary Hamel and C. K. Prahalad. They defined a business's core competencies as the combination of technologies and skills that a company used to provide customer benefits better than anyone else.

Here are some projects to consider as you Leverage Your Core Competencies.

Conduct a competency review—Ask yourself: Are your current core competencies enough for the future of your business? Do you need to acquire additional competencies? Consider the competencies needed to make the iPod the massive success it has been over the past few years. Here is a "computer" company that acquired or developed the competencies to negotiate with music companies, design and engineer consumer electronic devices, and write new device-interface software to make it simple to download music via the Internet.

Consider partnering—Previously, business analysts believed that you should own the competencies that make your company unique and that you should outsource other work to those who do it better than you. The problem is that outsourcing became seen as a means of cost-containment, not as a path to competitive advantage. Great partners may not be the lowest-cost partners—they might bring other strengths you need. Review your suppliers, and see which of them should be considered partners because of the competencies they bring.

Transformation Group (New Customers / New Assets)

STRATEGY 10: DECLARE VICTORY AND MOVE ON

Sometimes you've taken a business as far as it can go. Now may be the time to think about a move that brings you to new places. Even if your existing business is mature and on the verge of decline, you have time to use it as a platform for future growth. Here are some projects to consider when you Declare Victory and Move On.

Find your exit—It's one thing to declare victory; it's another matter to actually find a buyer for the "old" business. Test the market and look at the possibilities that will allow you to declare victory. Can you sell your business? Can you find an underwriter for an IPO (initial public offering) and become a shareholder rather than the owner? How will you profitably exit the business so that you can move on to your next endeavor?

Study adjacencies—If you consider your existing business as the core of future possibilities, you can examine those channels, geographies, products, or even different businesses that are close to your existing business. However, you will need to look a bit further afield than you have done in the past since the adjacencies you have already examined have not been sufficient to renew the business.

Use your talent—Your existing business may have hit a dead-end for reasons outside of your control. However, you have the talent and the experience to start over. Steve Jobs was relieved of his position by Apple in 1985. He then went on to found NeXT Computer, and in 1986 he purchased Pixar for $10 million. When he sold Pixar to Disney for $7.4 billion in 2006, he became Disney's largest shareholder with 7 percent of their outstanding shares. Oh, and he still found time to rejoin Apple as its CEO in the late 1990s.

STRATEGY 11: KEEP THE KNOWLEDGE, SWITCH THE BUSINESS

This is the strategy of the serial entrepreneur who, like the Energizer Bunny, goes on and on and on. This is a more difficult strategy for a large company but a natural strategy for the small business owner with drive and flexibility. Consider some of the following projects as you contemplate how to Keep the Knowledge, Switch the Business.

Hold an after-action review—Your existing strategy may be working well or may have failed. Consider the four questions at the heart of a military after-action review and apply it to your business: 1) What did you want to achieve? 2) What did you achieve? 3) Why were your desired outcomes and your actual outcomes different? 4) What did you learn?

Carry out a goal analysis—Make sure you separate the means from the ends you are trying to achieve. Your goals should be specific, measurable, achievable, relevant, and time-based—take the time to develop and document appropriate goals. Once you have done so, you can build your plan for achieving these goals.

Develop a vision—What will long-term success look like? Can you see it in your mind's eye and, more importantly, can you explain it to others? If you can't, how will you get others to follow your lead? Corporate vision was a consulting hot button in the early 1990s and, subsequently, fell into disfavor. Spend the time and energy to do this well—it's worth it.

STRATEGY 12: CASH OUT AND DOUBLE DOWN

Many companies have business units or product lines that have seen better days and have little chance of revival. Emotionally, we often want to save them because of their past glory. But you have to ask yourself if that is the best use of your resources and talent. More often than not, the answer is an emphatic "No." Projects to consider for Cash out and Double Down include:

Do a lifecycle analysis—Ask yourself where each of your units stands on the lifecycle curve. Filco Automotive was a manufacturer and distributor of automotive electronic after-market products. Given the market conditions and the changes in technology, their land and building were worth more than the business. They sold everything and invested the proceeds in their small sheet metal operation in Phoenix that supplied Boeing with parts.

Create a business portfolio analysis—Look at your portfolio of businesses and assess market growth and market conditions. What should you prune from your portfolio, and where should you invest the proceeds?

As you consider your situation and the strategies that might best apply to you, make a list of the projects you need to undertake to make your strategy a reality for your organization. Start with the sample projects we have given you and add others as you see fit.

Secure

Once you have identified the projects you need, you must fund them. This is what happens in the secure step.

Developing a renewal strategy is hard work but often fun, since you can play "what if" to your heart's content. However, the cold light of day comes as you start to consider the allocation of hard and soft assets needed to make the strategy a reality. As you secure your resources, you need to keep in mind the yin and yang of executing your renewal strategy.

THE YIN AND YANG OF RENEWAL
Up to this point you have tasked yourself and others with the work of renewal and have a clear idea of what should be

done with your customers, product lines, or business. You may have decided to make changes to your portfolio of customers or your portfolio of assets or both. Now you have to "pull the trigger" and execute your intention.

It would be wonderful if effective execution followed seamlessly from strategic intention, but all of us know that is not typically the case. The management team, with input from key members of the workforce, has developed the overarching renewal strategy. But now the details have to be developed and implemented by the entire organization. Emotional and cultural issues will arise and you will be faced with the challenging work of leading projects where nearly everyone in your organization is a stakeholder.

Success requires that your renewal intention (strategy plus goals) and your execution (implementation of that strategy) match as seamlessly as possible if you are to avoid wasting time, talent, and resources. The concept of yin and yang is a reminder that you *must* take execution into consideration as you develop your strategy.

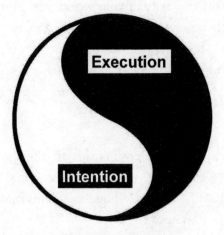

The Yin and Yang of Success

Making this even more difficult is the fact that everyone in your organization is already busy. This brings up the single largest challenge in executing renewal—how can you renew your business while everyone is busy running your business?

When we ask our clients to list some of the barriers to repositioning, this is what they tell us:

- There is no consensus on the need to renew.
- There is no time scheduled for renewal.
- Our leaders are close to retirement and are not willing to make changes to the business.
- We are fixated on what is right in front of us and don't discuss renewal.
- We can't take the risk of missing a quarterly earnings target.
- Concern over cannibalization delays renewal efforts.
- There is great urgency in the day-to-day, but renewal feels less urgent.

Execution is the point at which the reality of impending changes hits the majority of your workforce. Some will gladly go along with renewal; some will balk at the challenges in front of them. You will need to deal with conflicting values, insufficient information, and experts who disagree. Leadership at this point requires that you emphasize three aspects of renewal:

1. Clearly articulate the problems with the current state of the business and help the organization come to grips with the need to renew. People have to realize that renewal is a necessity, not an option.

2. Present a vision of the renewed organization. It may not be accepted by all, but it must be understood and accepted by a large percentage of your customers, partners, and workforce.
3. Formulate a plan with enough detail to move the organization into the future. You must let people know in broad terms what will be different for the organization, and what it will mean for their jobs.

With these three aspects of renewal in mind, it's time to consider the job of running the projects needed to implement your strategy.

THINKING ABOUT PROJECTS

What came to mind as you read the word *projects* in the heading? Did you think of technical aspects of project planning like PERT charts and bar charts and resource needs? If so, then you thought about the easy stuff.

We have been involved with projects for most of our careers. We have served as members of project teams, project leaders, decision makers, and now as teachers and coaches of renewal efforts. And over the years we have come to realize that successful business projects have three major characteristics: competent technical management, organizational savvy, and awareness of behavioral issues.

Technical Management

When it comes to the component of technical management, we suggest that you consider the models and teachings from the Project Management Institute, which has become the gold standard of expert knowledge over the past twenty or so years. If you need background and training, we refer you to the institute (*www.PMI.org*) and its books and learning guides.

We do, however, have four overarching observations.

1. You will need a full-time project manager for most renewal projects. Renewal is not a matter of tinkering around the edges; more often than not you will be making significant changes to your business, and you can't afford to have this managed on a part-time, *ad hoc* basis.

2. Plan the renewal implementation in enough detail so that you can track it on a week-to-week basis. Unfortunately, project plans are often looked upon as "necessary evils" that can be ignored after they have been presented to senior management. However, if done right, your project plan will become *the* basis for communications as the organization does the work of renewal.

3. Provide adequate resources for the renewal effort. Now is not the time to try to starve the organization into prosperity. Also, be realistic about the workload of the people assigned to the project. More often than not, we pile more work onto our best people without ever creating a "to stop doing" list for them. Now is the perfect time to create that list.

4. Set explicit and appropriate deadlines. Furthermore, hold individuals accountable for meeting those deadlines. We wish we didn't have to state the obvious, but all too often deadlines are viewed as movable suggestions rather than strategically important milestones.

Remember that project managers are constantly juggling constraints of time, budget, and scope. What deadlines have you set for renewal and are they hard and fast? Can the deadlines move up or back if circumstances change? How much money have you allocated for renewal? Will you still fund the future of the business if times get tough? Finally, can you adjust the scope of your renewal effort or is it "all or nothing"?

Keep in mind the reality of project life. If one constraint changes, something else will have to change as well. For example, cutting budget will affect timing or scope. With that in mind, make it clear to the organization which of the three constraints is "sacred." They will then know where they have room to maneuver.

Organizational Savvy

There is no doubt that renewal can (and will) upset the organizational apple cart. Make a list of the stakeholders in the renewal project and plot them along two axes: organizational power and level of support for the renewal. A stakeholder is anyone who can affect or is affected by the renewal projects. As you will discover, workers, families, suppliers, community, customers, and competitors are all stakeholders. And there will be more. Refer to the matrix on the following page. Think of all of your renewal stakeholders and see if you know in which box they fit.

As you consider your stakeholders, consider the following:

- Who will lose power and resources as part of the renewal?
- Who will gain power and resources as part of the renewal?
- Who are the opinion leaders the workforce will turn to for guidance?
- All projects have to deal with three major trade-offs: Time, Budget, and Scope. Is there organizational alignment as to which of these three is most important for the renewal effort?

As you proceed with the renewal make sure that you have a communication plan and a strategy for dealing with the concerns of all of your stakeholders.

Powerful stakeholders opposed to renewal	Powerful stakeholders in support of renewal
• • • • •	• • • • •
Weak stakeholders opposed to renewal	Weak stakeholders in support of renewal
• • • • •	• • • • •

Behavioral Issues

In our consulting work, company after company freely admits to us that projects are often late, or over budget, or completed with reduced scope, or all three! When we work with project managers during a project review we generally see that the issues are not technical, they are behavioral.

What separates the great intention underlying renewal project plans from great execution? Consider the seven items shown in the chart below.

Commitment
Conflict
Consequences
Measures
Resistance
Resources
Responsibility

Closing the Intention–Execution Gap

Commitment: Who *must* be intellectually and emotionally on board for renewal to succeed? Go back to the stakeholder matrix and consider the powerful stakeholders who are not in agreement with renewal. How could they scuttle the effort and what can you do to "move them to the right"? Don't confuse commitment with compliance. You need absolute commitment from some stakeholders and simple compliance from others.

Conflict: Conflict is healthy if it raises issues that have to be discussed and exposes trade-offs that should be made. Although it sounds nice, "win-win" seldom exists in the real world. Normally the best you can hope for is a "big win/little win," with one party realizing more of the benefit than the other.

Consequences: There will be organizational and personal consequences arising from renewal success or failure. Be clear about this early on and help stakeholders know how they might be affected. Education is your best course of action.

Measures: What financial measures will signal success or troubles? What customer measures will signal acceptance or rejection by the marketplace? What internal/operational measures can be used to track the effectiveness and efficiency of your efforts? And, finally, how will you measure (and capture) the learning that is taking place so that you can correct your course if needed?

Resistance: Most people do *not* resist change—they resist "being changed." As you embark on your journey the workforce will want to know the *why* behind renewal more than anything else. And until they really understand the why you should expect resistance. You would resist too if you were in their shoes.

Put it this way, if you were told to walk into a darkened room, would you move slowly or stride boldly into the room? You'd move slowly until someone turned the lights on. Explaining the why behind renewal is how you turn the organizational lights on.

Resources: What tangible and intangible resources are needed? Do you have the needed skills within the company or are you trying to wing it with your existing team? Depending on the strategy that you have chosen for renewal you may find that you need significant changes in your knowledge-based resources as well as your physical resources.

Responsibility: Now is the time to be as specific as possible regarding roles and responsibilities for the entire team. If everyone is deemed answerable for the success of the renewal effort, then no one will feel accountable on a personal level.

Switch

Transitioning from today's business model to the new business model may be easy for some of the strategies we have identified. The strategies associated with New Concepts and Extensions are relatively mild in terms of changes to the existing asset base and workers. Solutions strategies are a bit tougher on everyone as they require new assets and capabilities. Transformation strategies can be gut wrenching. Historically, businesses have handled these kinds of switches in various ways:

- *Separate the mature and the new business*—In the early 1980s, IBM placed its new PC business in Boca Raton, Florida, to physically remove it from the cultural pressures of the "big iron" (mainframe) business.
- *Start the old and renewed units together, but take them apart*— Internet start-ups within mature businesses often need the support of an established overhead structure until they get rolling. Then they need to be on their own so they can be measured properly. Tesco, the UK's biggest supermarket chain started Tesco.com in the mid-1990s to allow for online ordering of groceries. By 2003, the online unit was spun off so it could expand into Internet ordering (and subsequent delivery) of a much wider range of products.

- *Keep them under the same roof*—Intel's Dual-Core chips are high end; its Celeron chips are mid-range; and the new Atom chips are low and slow. But all these units stay under one business roof because of the similarity in competencies, facilities, and equipment needed to design and manufacture them.

The odds of trouble-free renewal are not very great. How can you minimize the problems that will almost inevitably occur? Here's our advice.

- Stay focused and be aware of conflicting priorities.
- Keep intention and execution aligned.
- Measure progress and take early corrective action.
- Involve your key stakeholders.
- Stay attuned to market changes.

The next chapter will cover the common traps we have found as companies employ the Rethink, Reinvent, Reposition process.

CHAPTER NINE

Avoiding Traps along the Way

As we've explored the renewal process, we've come to feel that it's logical and intuitive. Each step flows from the previous one. So why don't more organizations, both large and small, make a successful transition to a renewed business? We think the main reason is that they fall into traps along the way. We have identified a dozen of the most common traps for a business on its way to renewal and will cover them in this chapter.

•

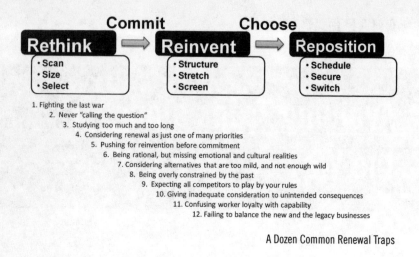

Commit → **Choose**

Rethink ⇒ **Reinvent** ⇒ **Reposition**
- Scan
- Size
- Select

- Structure
- Stretch
- Screen

- Schedule
- Secure
- Switch

1. Fighting the last war
   2. Never "calling the question"
      3. Studying too much and too long
         4. Considering renewal as just one of many priorities
            5. Pushing for reinvention before commitment
               6. Being rational, but missing emotional and cultural realities
                  7. Considering alternatives that are too mild, and not enough wild
                     8. Being overly constrained by the past
                        9. Expecting all competitors to play by your rules
                           10. Giving inadequate consideration to unintended consequences
                              11. Confusing worker loyalty with capability
                                 12. Failing to balance the new and the legacy businesses

A Dozen Common Renewal Traps

Remember, forewarned is forearmed. You don't *have* to fall into any of these traps, but you do have to know about them in advance.

Trap 1: Fighting the Last War

Historians often criticize generals who "fought the last war." Simply put, such generals had a very intense experience in one context and neglected to consider how the new war will not be like the old war. This curse of past knowledge afflicts all leaders—you know too much about your existing business and forget to see the world anew. Experience, the very thing that is valuable in running a business (or a war, in the case of generals) can become an impediment when the rules change. Rather than fall back on the old rules, it's best to spend the time thinking about the reality of the current situation and how it will evolve in the coming years.

Record companies were guilty of fighting the last war when online music sharing became rampant. They had historically made money selling CDs, and fought to protect these sales by suing their customers for illegal downloading. They didn't see that physical CDs were the last war, and developing a business model for online music is the next war.

Some thoughts for you to consider:

- Have you built future-based competencies into your workforce?
- Are you assuming that your loyal customers will always remain loyal to you?
- Are you devoting effort to appealing to the next generation?

The fact is, too often company leadership uses the same tactics and strategies they employed years before to deal with *today's* problems. And that just doesn't work. You must be willing to look at your opportunities from the point of view of your customers, your competitors, and your junior leaders and be ready to challenge your own thinking.

We suggest that you put aside some time to wrestle with two very important questions.

1. What don't you know about the situation that you should? (This is *not* the time to pretend that you know it all!)
2. What assumptions are you making, based on past experience, that may no longer hold true?

Trap 2: Never "Calling the Question"

The status quo can feel just fine for a long time, assuming the changes to your industry are gradual. Many product lines or business units that you should consider for renewal are currently the "cash cows" of your main business and, frankly, can be comfortable to operate. The vast majority of the big operating decisions have already been made, and with assets in place, cash flow may still be quite strong. It's tempting to assume that this situation will continue indefinitely. If you were Blockbuster in the early 2000s, would you have foregone the profits in videocassette and DVD rentals to investigate making money from movie downloads?

When organizations fall into this trap, they often find that they have sacrificed future success in order to keep the present organization healthy. Pundits like to point out the foolishness of business leaders when they "miss the future." However, as it has been remarked many times, hindsight is 20–20. Business leaders are charged with making decisions often based on imperfect information. So what is the decision maker to do?

First, make sure you pay attention to the trends and warning signs on the edge of your mental radar screen. Remember, life-cycles are inevitable, and although you may have had a good run, nothing lasts forever. Second, commit to the long-term health of your business. You must be willing to face the brutal facts regarding trade-offs you need to make as you balance actions today with their future effects. Third, muster the courage to raise the tough issues on a regular basis. We suggest that questions of renewal be raised at least annually for any ongoing business.

Trap 3: Studying Too Much and Too Long

Some forms of renewal are riskier than others, but all entail a degree of personal and organizational risk. Ideally, we would like to be able to *prove* to all relevant stakeholders that the decision we are about to make is the right one. And so we try to find as much data and do as much analysis as possible. The problem with this approach is that *there are no facts about the future*. You have no choice but to use judgment to fill the voids in your knowledge.

You have to sense industry changes, make sense of them, and decide on a course of action fast enough to keep up with them. Otherwise your organization becomes irrelevant. One of the authors invested in an online calendar company in the early dot com days. As his company prepared to launch by refining and adding additional features, competitor after competitor launched their own calendar offerings. By the time his company was finally ready to go the early competitors had already locked up the market.

Renewal and the decisions it brings with it do not have precise and correct answers. Rather they require solid managerial judgment within the time available. You will never be able to prove ahead of time which renewal alternative is the best. Just do the best job you can do in the time available.

Trap 4: Considering Renewal as Just One of Many Priorities

Leadership teams are continuously burdened with myriad competing priorities. Although renewal may make it to the top of the list, all too often there are insufficient resources devoted to it because there are too many other ongoing initiatives. Should you spend the time and effort on renewal, or should you grab some "low-hanging fruit"?

We recognize the challenge of keeping a business alive so that you can get to the future. We suggest that you also consider the need to get to the right future. Doing so takes time and leadership focus. But with the lean organizations of today, where will time and focus come from?

Think about this for a second. Over the past fifteen or more years companies all over the world have saved their bottom line by attacking operating costs. Being lean and mean is a drumbeat that all of us have heard, especially during the recent recession. Unfortunately, many organizations have relegated renewal and reflecting on the future of the business to the "get to it someday" category of work.

Our advice on how to avoid this trap is going to sound like heresy. We suggest that you allow some *in*efficiency in your organization and allow managers and leaders at all levels a bit of time to ponder the future of the organization and what it will take to get there. You need a bit of adaptive capacity if you are going to lead a system that can adjust itself to the reality of a changing environment.

3M has done this for years. Their engineers and scientists are allotted a day a week to work on innovation. Google does the same thing and estimates 50 percent of its innovations come from this "free time."

Trap 5: Pushing for Reinvention before Commitment

You may clearly sense the need for renewal and want to move as quickly as possible to the Reposition phase. However, you may find yourself leading a parade that has no participants. The decision to tackle serious renewal is rarely made by one person.

Even the head of a family-owned business has to live with the reality of buy-in. You need to convince the leadership of the necessity and wisdom of the change before they will help you implement it.

Daryl Conner, the change-management consultant and writer, explains that three conditions are necessary for organizational change to take hold:

1. Dissatisfaction with the status quo.
2. A vision of the future.
3. A plan to get from the present condition to the desired state.

Early on, however, dissatisfaction with the status quo is rarely obvious to all stakeholders. You must make them aware of the case for renewal and convince them of its validity. If you try to carry out renewal while bypassing your executive team, you'll pay a heavy price later on.

Trap 6: Being Rational, but Missing Emotional and Cultural Realities

There is no doubt that you should estimate the cost of the renewal effort and what you might expect in returns on that effort. However, this is not simply a run-the-numbers exercise. As you think about the entirety of renewing your business, think about the balance between intention and execution. Under the heading of intention are the goals and plans of renewal, which will primarily come from the rational side of your brain. You will ask and try to answer questions such as "What is and will be our market share?" "How much will this cost?" "Do we have the cash reserves?"

However, the execution side of the reinvention effort depends heavily on the emotional buy-in of the managers and workers. You must be able to make renewal happen within the existing business culture, often while building a new culture for the renewed business.

One of the authors has conducted workshops on project leadership for years and generally starts each workshop by asking for a list of the reasons projects have failed in the past. Here are some of the answers he gets time and time again. Note how many are rooted in the culture of the company:

- Poor communication
- Hidden agendas
- A sense of winners and losers
- Micromanagement
- Ignoring stakeholders
- Not explaining the *why* behind the project
- Not communicating a vision

We recommend that you create a tailored list of why projects fail at your organization and then develop a list of answers to address each source of failure. Remember, when strategy and culture disagree, culture usually trumps strategy.

Trap 7: Considering Alternatives That Are Too Mild and Not Enough Wild

Reinvention can be quite uncomfortable, and therefore, leaders often consider a limited (and standard) set of alternatives.

But most smaller changes have been tried already and have not been sufficient to successfully renew the organization. Mild is defensible. Mild is reasonable. But mild won't make a significant change to the organization.

Organizations don't like wild. After all, wild may not work. What organizations do like is control. This is where strong leadership is needed. In the words of car racing legend Mario Andretti: "If everything seems under control, you're just not going fast enough." If you try to control everything, you will never stretch far enough, or go fast enough, to successfully renew your business.

Because the changes you're proposing are fundamental ones, it's essential that you get strong commitment from your team. Obtaining surface agreement but not getting deep commitment will haunt you during the implementation phase. This results in "malicious compliance" in which people don't directly fight the change, but they do nothing to make the change happen.

Earlier we mentioned that running a mature business can be very comfortable. Your executive team may agree with the need to renew, but they may not be excited about the difficulty the journey will entail. Anyone who has worked in a large organization (and many small organizations as well) has had experience with the "corporate nod." Agreement seems at hand, but you know that hearts and minds are not truly engaged. Their heads get it, but their hearts are not in it. It's your responsibility to energize the team and push them out of their comfort zones. You will need to help them visualize the rewards that can come with embracing the "Wild."

Trap 8: Being Overly Constrained by the Past

Although this is similar to Fighting the Last War, it differs in that the past can often affect the entire organization. Your whole business or industry can fall in love with what it does and fail to see what is happening around them. A classic example is how the railroad industry neglected to see the opportunities in interstate trucking because the railroad companies conceived of themselves as "railroads" instead of "transportation" businesses. More recently, oil companies have focused on their ability to find, extract, and refine oil and have neglected customers' emerging needs for reliable and cost-efficient energy.

The weight of history is particularly heavy on smaller firms that were started by charismatic or iconic founders. Though his day may be long gone, the founder's name is often used as an explanation for why something new cannot be tried. "The old man would roll over in his grave if he thought we were seriously considering this!"

Trap 9: Expecting All Competitors to Play by Your Rules

Sometimes an industry gives a wink and a nod to norms about offerings, customer relations, and speed of change. In the U.S. auto industry through much of the twentieth century, the Big Three—Ford, GM, and Chrysler—set annual style changes, followed a bigger-is-better philosophy, and decided on what they regarded as reasonable quality levels for their products. But in the 1970s, the Japanese came into the market, playing by different rules. It was the beginning of a long period of decline for the American auto industry, one that continues today.

AT&T and the Baby Bells made enormous investments in fixed phone lines. Replicating this investment would cost billions, so it seemed they were insulated from competition. That is, until upstart companies began using Voice Over Internet Protocol (VoIP) to make phone calls at almost no variable cost and without having to invest significant capital.

Avoiding this trap requires you to occasionally think like an outsider. Look at your actions and the actions of your competitors and ask yourself if they make sense. Would a new entrant analyze your actions and see a strategic weakness to exploit? If so, you may be playing by rules that no longer apply.

Trap 10: Giving Inadequate Consideration to Unintended Consequences

Once a leader has chosen the best alternative and embarked on the journey of renewal, her focus is on the intended consequences of the decision. However, all solutions create new problems, and the problems often arise in a different time and place. Here are some examples for you to ponder:

- You may not devote proper attention to your existing customers as you move the spotlight to your new best friends. Your assumptions about the loyalty of your best customers may prove to be woefully weak.
- Existing suppliers could worry about their place in the new scheme of things. They might preempt your move to possibly

replace them by finding new customers of their own, leaving your supply chain less secure.

- A change in performance metrics, while right for the long-term, might result in missed short-term rewards for key workers and, consequently, lower morale. It might seem like a smart move to compensate employees according to your company's stock price. But what if your stock price plummets and everyone's options become so far out of the money that morale is destroyed?

To avoid this trap, take the time to consider the *what ifs* of anticipated changes to your business. Think of some long chains of cause and effect and look for problems that you might create in the name of renewal.

Trap 11: Confusing Loyalty with Capability

Most leaders have a cadre of loyal followers. They follow the leader from job to job and from company to company. However, the renewal of a business depends more on the capabilities of the team conducting the work than on the loyalty of the team members. We are not recommending that you become heartless and unfeeling, but you must make sure that loyalty does not get in the way of obtaining the competencies you need for success. If you really want to help your team, do whatever it takes to craft a successful future for the business.

Who do you put in charge of the new business? Too often people install a "good company person" who has put in some years and is well thought of within the legacy firm. But that person may lack the characteristics required to succeed in the new business. When push comes to shove, you must go with the people who can win, not those who have been around the longest.

This issue is critical for family-owned businesses. A charismatic founder starts with nothing and builds a business. He turns it over to his daughter who maintains it. She then passes the business on to her modestly talented son who promptly drives it into the ground.

We have identified eight capabilities a leader needs to be effective. They are:

- Observing
- Reasoning
- Imagining
- Challenging
- Deciding
- Learning
- Enabling
- Reflecting

All are obvious, but not all are used regularly. Our consulting work has identified Challenging, Imagining, and Reflecting as three underused capabilities. During the renewal effort make sure you have people who are willing to challenge the present business and its assumptions, who can imagine a future business model, and who will take the time to reflect on ongoing success and challenges. Loyalty is desired, but capabilities are required.

Trap 12: Failing to Balance the New and the Old Businesses

If you are renovating the existing business by improving and expanding the current customer or upgrading business assets, matters are relatively simple, since the business as a whole is involved. However, there may be renewal efforts that affect only one portion of the business. If this is the case, you will have to continue the old business, possibly managing it through a graceful decline, while simultaneously growing the new business.

If you give the old business too large a share of your resources, you detract from the launch of the renewed business. If you starve the old business, you run the risk of killing it prematurely and losing the cash flow you need to support the renewal effort.

Energy companies, for example, currently divide their time between oil exploration and alternative energy research and development. But time, attention, and resources are limited, even for rich oil companies. Their leaders must decide how to split their resources between the two activities so they maintain healthy cash flows while searching for tomorrows successes.

We wish we had a foolproof formula for avoiding this trap, but we don't. You'll have to make a judgment call that will depend on the boldness of your renewal effort and the capabilities at your disposal. That said, here is some general advice:

- Make sure your entire team understands and accepts the speed at which things are evolving. Is your existing business in gradual or steep decline? Now look at the renovated business. Do you have to move quickly and boldly or can you take some time?

- Know your goals. You have to know where you are and where you want to go with *both* the renewed business and the business in decline. Measuring both with the same set of metrics will cause you to feed one and starve the other.
- Have fallback positions because things *will* go wrong. Now is not the time to substitute hope or luck for good planning. You need an organization that can detect, contain, and bounce back from the unavoidable setbacks all renewal efforts encounter.
- Be flexible in dealing with emotional and cultural issues. The business unit in decline needs your understanding. The business unit in early growth needs your encouragement.
- Protect the people you want to keep who work in the legacy business. Let them know they will still have a job with you even after the legacy business has gone away.

CHAPTER TEN

Building Renewal Capabilities in the Next Generation of Leaders

We have explained the differences in the leadership talent and abilities required as a business transitions through the various stages of its lifecycle. Growing a business needs skills that are different than those needed to run a mature business. Likewise, renewing a business needs different abilities than running a business. A major challenge comes from the fact that the mature stage of a business can last for a very long time, and therefore, the capabilities needed to run a mature business are often considered the norm. But even long-run maturity is simply a stage through which every business will pass on its way to renewal or decline.

Leaders learn lessons along the way and benefit from their experiences, both good and bad. What can you do to pass on these lessons to the emerging leaders in your organization? How can you build their renewal skills? To be able to lead a renewal effort, they must move from executing strategy to leading in its development.

The Responsibilities of Every Business Leader

Every business leader, no matter the type or size of business they lead, is faced with six very basic responsibilities. They are:

1. *To understand and communicate the vision, values, and goals of the organization.* This lies at the heart of every strategy the business adopts, including renewal. The collective message behind vision, values, and goals lays the foundation for what a business will or will not achieve. The local dry cleaner owner who sees herself as simply running a shop will not look for other opportunities in or beyond her neighborhood. But her sister, with aspirations for a chain of establishments, will scour new neighborhoods for expansion opportunities. The vision for a business, if it is understood and embraced by the organization, becomes the magnetic north and guides all strategic decisions.

2. *To sense the signals of tomorrow.* Today's problems and opportunities sit before us with terrible clarity; tomorrow's problems and opportunities are hazy and indistinct. But if we don't take time to adapt to and anticipate future conditions, we will not have sufficient time to react. Starbucks grew phenomenally throughout the 1990s. What if Folgers Coffee had sensed the changes in the U.S. coffee culture sooner? What might they have done before Starbucks set the pace? On the other hand, did the leaders at Starbucks anticipate the impact that the 2008–09 economic downturn would have on discretionary spending? If they had, would they have added locations as fast as they did or would they have set themselves a more measured pace?

3. *To make sense of these signals in light of the business's vision, values, and goals.* Sensing the signals of tomorrow is not enough. You have to consider the potential impact of their reality on your business. Is it a problem or an opportunity coming at you? Is it something you can ignore or is it a game-changer for your industry? What assumptions have you made in the past that may no longer hold true? Think about mainstream retailing in the mid-1970s. Sears, JCPenney, and Montgomery Ward were the "big three," and they dominated the department store category in the United States. By focusing on what they did best and by considering only each other as competitors they missed the dual shifts toward discounting and specialty shops.

   The work of making sense of the signals often doesn't really look like work. After all, you're "just" thinking about things. The danger here is that your people neglect to spend time thinking because they need to look busy.

4. *To decide on a course of action in a timely manner.* It's not enough to anticipate tomorrow and to make sense of the potential changes. Action is required, and that means you have to decide on changes to your business. Family-owned businesses often wait too long to determine who will follow Pops now that Pops is old and sick. Many founders/owners don't want to cause family strife by naming a successor (or giving her real power) and they delay until it's too late. Yes, decision making is risky, and you might make a mistake. However, no progress can be made until someone makes a decision and moves the business forward.

5. *To act on the decision.* Most organizations deny themselves the full value of their decisions by underestimating the resources necessary for execution and adding more onto the managers' existing to-do lists than they can ever accomplish. This results in a significant gap between the intention behind and the execution of our business decisions. And that is one of the main reasons so many mature businesses fail to renew themselves in time.

6. *To be prepared to do it all over again.* Renewal is not a one-time effort. Industries are evolving faster than ever and leaders are going to have to consider the realities of renewal again and again. This may not be comfortable, but it is necessary. If you fall behind the pace of industry change, you risk becoming an also-ran as your competitors pull away from you.

We want to close this book with some ideas about how to develop an organization that is capable of sensing and responding to the ongoing need to renew. It is much easier to work on renewing 10 percent of the organization each year than it is to totally renew once every ten years. Massive renewal may be "heroic," but ongoing renewal is smart.

As we thought about the challenge of building an organization capable of renewing itself we looked across past clients, past experiences, and industries and companies we have studied and asked two simple questions: Where have we seen this capability consistently in action, and what kinds of organizations seem consistently capable of renewal? Two types of organizations operating in different dynamic environments came to mind almost immediately: the U.S. military and professional services firms.

How the U.S. Military Develops the Next Generation of Leaders

The U.S. military has a rigorous process for developing young leaders. Those who will be first sergeants in 2025 are low-ranking enlisted men and women today. As you read this book, the Army generals of tomorrow are sitting in West Point. However, the wars and conflicts of the future will be different from those we are conducting today. The world is changing and the military must keep up. So how does military leadership prepare the men and women who will have to deal with an unknown future?

Lt. General William Lennox was superintendent of the U.S. Military Academy at West Point when he was interviewed for a 2005 issue of *Leader to Leader*. In the interview he was asked about the biggest challenge for the leadership of West Point. He spoke about the young cadets at West Point and responded, "I don't know where these young people are going to be five, ten, fifteen years in the future, so we have to teach them *how* to think, not *what* to think."

Lennox knows that change is on the horizon and accepts that he does not know what it is. With that as a given, the focus of preparation has shifted from teaching past best practices to enabling the cadets to think for themselves about the fog of war.

Now consider your organization and the reality of your competitive environment. Do you know the *what* and *where* of future competition and industry evolution? We doubt that you do as you look out more than a few years.

The military, more than any organization, has to constantly renew its competencies in response to challenges across the globe. After all, they deal with life-and-death situations in the reality of geopolitics. Where will they fight next? Who will be their opponent? Military leaders must consider the future of warfare and prepare the troops as best they can today.

How does the military prepare its emerging leaders? It can't wait until someone is a general or an admiral before giving him or her responsibilities. Consider the following points and see if any of them could apply to your situation as you think about preparing your next generation of leaders for the renewal challenges they will face.

- Young military leaders are expected at all times to stay aware of not only their immediate mission and objectives but also the bigger strategic picture. They are prepared to step in for their superiors if need be. Can you say the same thing for the emerging leaders in your organization? Do they know the mission and objectives of your business? Do they understand your long-term goals and strategies? Could they fill in for you if needed?
- Young military leaders are given authority early and are expected to make decisions and live with them from the very beginning of their career. Do your senior executives give enough opportunities to young business leaders? Are your managers inclined to "delegate upward" and avoid the responsibility of making tough decisions?
- In addition to accepting responsibility, young leaders in the military are mentored by more experienced officers and noncommissioned officers. It's in the best interest of the young leaders to listen to their advice. Young leaders may

have the knowledge; they also need the collective wisdom of those who have been around the block a few times. Does your upper management mentor young, up-and-coming executives?

- Young military leaders are tested regularly, both physically and mentally. Performance reviews in the military are a vehicle for solid development. Does your company make the best use of its reviews? Or do managers view them as something to be dreaded or as a hoop through which to jump?

- In the military, young leaders are required to take responsibility for the results of their units. If the unit is successful, it gets credit. If the unit fails, the leader takes the heat. In your company, do the leaders accept responsibility for the performance of their team?

- Young officers often work with and assist senior leaders. It helps them think bigger and it gives them the opportunity to see more experienced leaders in action. How often do the senior executives of your company invite junior leaders into their strategic conversations?

Of course, you are not a general getting ready for war. You're a business leader getting ready for the future. What could you learn from the military and the way it prepares junior leaders that might help you with your business? Our recommendations are presented later in this chapter but here is our initial challenge: Are you developing managers of the status quo in your organization or are you actively trying to develop leaders? It's not a trivial question—consider it seriously.

Faster Than the Speed of Evolution

Consider the problems faced by professional services firms. They have to sense emerging issues, both good and bad, and quickly make sense of those issues in the context of their clients' needs and their own abilities to build the right competencies. Professional service firms live and die by exceeding the speed of industry evolution. Their clients, operating in dynamic environments, need firms that are either right with them or, better yet, slightly ahead of them. And given the speed of change in many industries, professional service firms can't afford to wait for the senior partners to figure things out. They figure things out on the front line in the field in real-time.

David Maister is a top consultant to professional service firms. In his book *True Professionalism* he identified a dozen critical business processes of a professional service firm. Seven of the processes we think apply directly to the issue of renewal:

- Developing innovative approaches to solving client problems
- Turning individual client assignments into long-term relationships
- Continuously gathering market intelligence and tracking emerging client needs
- Generating awareness of capabilities in important markets
- Developing new services
- Transferring skills to junior professionals
- Disseminating and sharing skills and knowledge among partners

Read the list again and think of the individual capabilities needed to enable these processes. "Developing innovative approaches" requires staff members who understand and can act like entrepreneurs. "Building long-term relationships" requires good emotional intelligence. "Gathering market intelligence" requires research capabilities. You get the idea—every one of these processes requires a unique set of capabilities in both existing and emerging leaders.

These business processes are central to renewal no matter what kind of business you run—from a family-owned shop to a division of a global multinational. No matter what your situation, you must train your up-and-coming leaders in the skills listed above.

People grow fastest when they are challenged. Many professionals are used to being challenged right from the beginning of their careers, and it doesn't let up as they move up. Think of your own people. Are they challenged? Or do they sit in meetings that are disorganized and going nowhere? Do they wade through stacks of irrelevant email? Do they wait for their bosses to get back to them on things they easily could have done themselves?

It should also be noted that, even with all of this effort to develop them, there are some professional service people who won't develop quickly enough or don't have the raw talent to succeed in the business.

In many companies, substandard performers would be kept on, diluting the overall staff. Even in recessionary times, layoffs are usually aligned with seniority, not skills. In contrast, top professional services firms lay off one out of every three people every three or four years. This is not a cost-cutting move, but a considered plan to continually upgrade the overall quality of staff at every level. Tough? You bet! But that's why you are willing to pay the big bucks to these firms. They really do have the best and the brightest.

Professional services firms have high standards, high accountability, and high rewards. The riskiest thing you can do in one of these firms is to not grow. Stagnation means loss of opportunity and job security. How would your organization evolve if it followed these same rules as it developed its next generation of leaders?

Renewal Takes More Than Brains

Whether it's for the military or a professional service firm, the renewal responsibilities of your next generation of leaders are straightforward and pretty easy to explain: they have to learn how to sense, to make sense, to decide, and to act; all in the context of your vision, values, and goals.

However, for all its simplicity and reasonableness, there is a fundamental renewal problem—organizations don't do it consistently. These capabilities *should* work as described, but they often break down in the real world.

There are three perspectives from which people look at any strategy, including renewal: rational, emotional, and cultural. The trick is getting all three to line up with one another. For example, a company might rationally want to grow profits by expanding into another field. Emotionally, this is a challenge since the company's leaders may have ignored or belittled this other field as not being worthy of their attention. Culturally, it may be a challenge because the company has always kept a narrow focus in everything it undertakes.

It's your job to get your emerging leaders to overcome their fears and concerns about your chosen renewal strategy. From a cultural standpoint (by far the hardest of the three elements to change), you might point out that growing the company will mean looking beyond traditional boundaries. You might implement specific steps (e.g., retreats, visits to other companies, etc.) that can start to change your culture. It is worth pointing out in this context that most company cultures are determined from the top downward, so you have to set the example if you want anything to change.

Consider the organizational renewal building that goes on in the military and in professional service firms. Now think about the work needed to keep your business in sync with industry evolution. Here are our suggestions for preparing your emerging leaders to drive future renewal efforts.

Rational View

Future leaders need to be able to analyze changes to the business in the context of emerging industry change and understand the implications of the changes. They must "think bigger than their job" because the answer to the question of "why?" is always in the environment outside the company. For example, a procurement manager might not understand why you want to upgrade logistics support software if she doesn't know about the need to integrate with global suppliers.

Future leaders need to understand the larger goals and the numerous ways of achieving those goals. Therefore, we suggest that you make a concerted effort to help your emerging leaders understand industry dynamics and how your business actually makes its money. The more they can see their jobs in the context of business results, the better they will be able to anticipate and appreciate industry evolution.

- Customers will determine the success of your business. Future leaders should be given every opportunity to build relationships with real customers, not just read summarized market data. Competitive truth is always found at the customer interface.
- Help emerging leaders develop their critical thinking skills. Ask them about their assumptions. Encourage them to look at situations from multiple points of view. Focus on their thinking skills more than their knowledge of today's tools and techniques.

Emotional View

We'd like to think of ourselves as "rational players" in the game of business. But we're more than that. We exhibit emotions even though many of us hesitate to speak of them.

- When business is simple we can rely on best practices because we can find the answers. Likewise, when business is specialized we can rely on experts because they know the answers. However, when business becomes complex we often have to rely on experimentation. Nobody knows the answers in advance and there is always the potential for failure. And in many organizations failure is seen as career limiting. If your future leaders are fearful of the impact that a failed experiment will have on their career, they will always go for the safe bets. You cannot prevent their fear, but you can help them put it in the proper perspective. If you're not sure about this, ask yourself: Is your business becoming *less* complex? We doubt it; so be prepared to help your emerging leaders undertake risky experiments.

- Business decisions take guts as well as brains because of the real potential of making a wrong call. None of us wants to fail, but it happens. So, expect future leaders to make small but meaningful decisions early in their career and then escalate the stakes as they progress. Renewal decisions can be bet-the-business decisions, and you want a cadre of people making these decisions who have been tested along the way. The only way people get good at making decisions is to do so early and often. Are your emerging leaders expected to make tough calls along the way, or do they simply wait for word to come down from the executive suite?

Cultural View

The easiest way to think about culture is to answer the question: How do we do things around here? You might think you are open to suggestions, but if your emerging leaders have learned not to disagree with you, you might misunderstand your corporate environment. Here's a suggestion. Get an outsider to ask your workers to identify the beliefs, values and norms that are used to run your organization on a daily basis. You might find you don't have the culture you thought you had or the one that you need to win in the future.

- Improvements to a business can take place within a functional silo. But these improvements will almost always be in conflict with other silos. For example, purchasing wants to buy in bulk because it lowers unit costs. But inventory control is tasked with keeping stocks at the lowest effective level and so may resist buying in bulk. Renewal is almost always broad and cross functional. Give your future leaders the opportunity (maybe even the mandate) to build cross-functional relationships and *use* multiple points of view. You have to network to get things done; help them develop their networks and their networking skills.

- Our strongest recommendation for developing new leaders is to build a *great* project management culture, a culture that deals realistically with the tradeoffs of budgets, deadlines, and deliverables. Think about this for a moment. Projects are the mechanism that businesses use to bring about the changes needed to execute strategy. Planning and leading projects gives young leaders the opportunity to build the skills they will need later in their career.

  They will have to make a suite of decisions during the course of the project. They will have to build relationships with temporary team members. They will almost always have to deal with cross-functional issues. And most importantly, they will have to learn to hold themselves accountable for the results they deliver.

Getting Ready for Tomorrow

If you are going to be ready for the challenges of tomorrow, you need to build the skills to Rethink, Reinvent, and Reposition early in the careers of your future leaders. If you want them to be prepared for the unknown and unknowable future facing most companies, you need to help them build the skills needed to:

- Think critically and strategically
- Reflect on reality
- Make good decisions
- Implement decisions effectively and efficiently

In this book we have discussed the process, tools, and skills required for successful renewal. To continue the conversation, go to *www.rethinkreinventreposition.com*. There you can ask questions, read through additional case studies, and submit your own ideas on renewal.

We wish you good luck, good fortune, and good renewal!

Resources for Further Reading

Books

Burns, Christopher. *Deadly Decisions: How False Knowledge Sank the Titanic, Blew Up the Shuttle, and Led America into War*. New York: Prometheus Books, 2008.

Charan, Ram, and Noel M. Tichy. *Every Business Is a Growth Business: How Your Company Can Prosper Year after Year*. New York: Times Books, 1998.

Christensen, Clayton M., Scott D. Anthony, and Erik A. Roth. *Seeing What's Next: Using the Theories of Innovation to Predict Industry Change*. Boston: Harvard Business School Publishing, 2004.

Day, George S., and Paul J. H. Schoemaker. *Peripheral Vision: Detecting the Weak Signals That Will Make or Break Your Company*. Boston: Harvard Business School Press, 2006.

Kim, W. Chan, and Renée Mauborgne. *Blue Ocean Strategy: How to Create Uncontested Market Space and Make the Competition Irrelevant*. Boston: Harvard Business School Publishing, 2005.

Penn, Mark J., with E. Kinney Zalesne. *Microtrends: The Small Forces behind Tomorrow's Big Changes*. New York: Twelve Hachette Book Group, 2007.

Plantes, Mary Kay, and Robert D. Finfrock. *Beyond Price: Differentiate Your Company in Ways That Really Matter*. Austin, TX: Greenleaf Book Group Press, 2009.

Welter, Bill, and Jean Egmon. *The Prepared Mind of a Leader: Eight Skills Leaders Use to Innovate, Make Decisions, and Solve Problems*. San Francisco: Jossey-Bass, 2006.

Zook, Chris. *Beyond the Core: Expand Your Market without Abandoning Your Roots*. Boston: Harvard Business School Publishing, 2004.

Articles

Amabile, Teresa. "How to Kill Creativity." HBR On Point, 2000.

Eisenhardt, Kahwajy, and Bourgeois. "How Management Teams Can Have a Good Fight." HBR On Point, 2000.

Garvin, David, and Michael Roberto. "What You Don't Know About Decision Making." HBR On Point, 2001.

Mankins, Michael C. "Stop Wasting Time." *Harvard Business Review*, September, 2004.

Index

Medical Library
North Memorial Health Care
3300 Oakdale Avenue North
Robbinsdale, MN 55422

Medical Library
North Memorial Health Care
3300 Oakdale Avenue North
Robbinsdale, MN 55422